DIGITAL DNA

Understanding and Developing Your Online Persona

* * * * *

This is for the bold soul building a business, or a brand on their own terms.

This journey is yours. And it's worth every step.

CONTENTS

ACKNOWLEDGEMENTS

No book is ever truly written alone. Even if the writing itself happens in late-night sessions fueled by caffeine, playlists, and a lot of head scratching. I'm deeply grateful to the people who made this journey not only possible, but meaningful.

First and foremost, to my amazing wife and Editor-in-Chief, Christie. Thank you for being my partner in every way. Your support, patience, and editorial eye kept this book (and me) on track. Every chapter is better because of you.

To my kids, thank you for inspiring me daily. You push me to be a better role model, not just in work, but in life. This book is part of the legacy I hope makes you proud.

To my team at Curiosity Marketing Group, you are the heartbeat of our execution and innovation. Your creative minds and strategic instincts have shaped not just this book, but so many wins we've celebrated together. Our success would not be what it is without you.

To my parents, thank you for the life you gave me and the example you set. The values, work ethic, and curiosity you nurtured laid the foundation for everything I do today.

And to the mentors, collaborators, and champions who've walked beside me over the years, whether you offered advice, challenged my thinking, or just showed up when I needed it, thank you. You've each helped shape this message and this moment.

I'm incredibly lucky to be surrounded by people who believe in growth, creativity, and purpose. This book may have my name on the cover, but its DNA belongs to all of us.

FOREWORD

What to expect from this book? Simple. We will try to make the creation, ownership, and maintenance of your Digital DNA as simple-and fun-as possible. If you're looking for a stiff corporate manifesto, you've picked the wrong book. If you want a practical, real-world guide from someone who's been in the trenches for decades? You're in the right place.

This book has been an arm wrestle for some time. For years, I've been nudged, poked, and flat-out begged to get the information out of my head and into a form others can use. Finally, here it is: the blueprint we've used time and again to help businesses (and people) build something credible, lasting, and truly them.

You'll be taken through a journey of what Digital DNA is, what it's made of, and how it can be leveraged. Whether you're running a well-oiled machine of a company, bootstrapping your first solo venture, or just trying to make sure your online presence doesn't scream "1997 called, it wants its website back," this book has something for you.

We'll cover the basics and the not-so-basics. From soul-searching your "why" to building out a brand that doesn't make you cringe. Discussing websites that actually convert to content that doesn't sound like AI wrote it on a coffee break. We'll even touch on the stuff most people ignore-like directory listings, reviews, and lead nurturing.

The goal? To leave you with a clear, actionable roadmap that helps you build, manage, and grow your online persona-your Digital DNA. Let's dive in!

Chapter 1

What is Digital DNA?

Let's start with a little myth-busting: Digital DNA is not just your website. It's not your Instagram aesthetic, how many connections you have on LinkedIn, or whether you remembered to update your Google Business profile this year (though, for the love of search rankings, please do that). Digital DNA is the full, interconnected web of who you are online-and more importantly, how people perceive you because of it.

Think of it like this: if someone Googled you or your business right now, what would they find? What story would those images, links, articles, profiles, and reviews tell? That story is your Digital DNA. It's not just data; it's your digital narrative. A hybrid of structure and personality. A mash-up of technology and tone. It's every single breadcrumb that leads people to decide who you are and whether they trust you.

The DNA Metaphor

Let's borrow from biology for a second. Just like your biological DNA determines your traits-eye color, height, that weird second toe-your Digital DNA shapes your online identity. It's a living, evolving sequence of visuals, signals, content, and context. It's how your brand breathes, speaks, and interacts on the web.

Where genes control how your body functions, your digital elements dictate how you're perceived. And in a world where 97% of people search online to find local businesses, perception is everything.

Imagine showing up to a job interview in a bathrobe and flip-flops. That's essentially what some brands do online. Broken links, blurry profile pictures, logos that look like they were made in MS Paint-these are the spinach-in-your-teeth moments of the digital world. Your Digital DNA should be clean, intentional, and consistent. It should represent the best version of you-because it's working 24/7, long after you've logged off.

The Building Blocks of Digital DNA

Let's break down what makes up your Digital DNA. These aren't just nice-to-haves-they're the core elements that shape your reputation, visibility, and success online:

- **Your Website** – This is your HQ, your flagship store, your digital office. Whether it's a clean one-pager or a robust e-commerce machine, it needs to load fast, be mobile-friendly, and clearly communicate your value. Fun fact: 42% of users will leave a website if it takes more than 3 seconds to load.

- **Social Media Profiles** – These are your brand's personalities at the digital party. Whether it's Instagram, TikTok, Twitter (or X, depending on your level of denial), consistency is key. Are you engaging with your audience or just posting into the void?

- **Directory Listings** – Google Business, Yelp, Healthgrades, TripAdvisor-whatever applies to your industry. These listings often make the first impression, especially in mobile searches. Keeping them accurate and up to date is critical.

- **Search Results** – Yep, Google yourself. Do it now. If your old Etsy shop, random YouTube comment, or outdated portfolio shows up first, it's time to course-correct. SEO matters.

- **Content** – Blogs, videos, podcasts, reels, tweets, LinkedIn articles. Every one of these is a puzzle piece in your bigger story. Inconsistent or missing content = missed opportunity.

- **Ratings & Reviews** – This is today's word-of-mouth marketing. 84% of people trust online reviews as much as personal recommendations. Enough said.

- **Micro Assets** – Email signatures, Zoom backgrounds, digital business cards, even the tone of your email auto-reply. These small touches stitch together a cohesive experience-or unravel it.

Each one of these elements is a thread. Individually, they matter. Together, they create the tapestry of your Digital DNA.

Why Digital DNA Matters More Than Ever

In the past, your first impression happened in a boardroom or over coffee. Today, it happens on screens. Before a single conversation, people will skim your profiles, check your reviews, scan your posts, and judge whether your digital footprint aligns with their expectations. And it happens fast: studies show people form an opinion about your site in just 0.05 seconds.

This is your handshake. Your elevator pitch. Your business card, billboard, and billboard-in-their-pocket all rolled into one. A polished Digital DNA helps you build trust faster, attract better leads, and show up stronger in a crowded market.

And this isn't just for brands with big ad budgets. Whether you're an entrepreneur, a nonprofit leader, a creative freelancer, or a corporate exec trying to build clout-your online presence is your reputation. It's how people decide if you're credible, consistent, and worth their time.

The Cost of Letting It Slide

Let's talk about what happens when your Digital DNA is a hot mess. Neglecting it doesn't just make you look sloppy-it actively costs you business:

- You lose leads because your contact form doesn't work, your phone number is wrong, or the "Book Now" button sends people to a 404 page. Every broken link is a broken opportunity.
- You confuse people when your Instagram says one thing, your website says another, and your LinkedIn hasn't been touched since pre-pandemic. Mixed messages breed hesitation, and hesitation kills conversions.
- You look untrustworthy if your last blog post is from 2018, your testimonials are vague or outdated, and your reviews are either nonexistent or full of unresolved complaints. Inconsistency = red flags.

- You vanish entirely when your directory listings are inconsistent. If your business name, address, or hours vary across platforms, Google starts to question your legitimacy. And when Google loses trust, so do your potential clients.
- You lose credibility when your visual brand is all over the place. One logo here, another font there, clashing colors everywhere. People associate visual chaos with lack of professionalism.
- You miss opportunities to show up in search results, in recommendations, and in the consideration set of your ideal customer. Outdated content and inactive profiles push you further down the digital food chain.

Think of it like digital decay. The longer you ignore it, the worse it gets. And unlike a messy garage, you can't just shut the door and pretend it doesn't exist. People are walking through it every day.

Taking Back Control

The good news? You don't need a PhD in computer science or a full-time agency to take control of your Digital DNA. You just need clarity, consistency, and a little guidance.

That's exactly what this book is for. We're going to break it down piece by piece. We'll walk through strategy and execution, the why and the how. We'll keep it real, keep it simple, and make sure every tactic serves a purpose.

This isn't about perfection. It's about presence. It's about showing up clearly, consistently, and with purpose.

But before you can build something great, you need to get clear on the foundation. Who are you trying to be online? What do you want people to feel, know, or do when they come across your brand?

That's where your Digital DNA begins. Let's build it-intentionally.

Chapter 2

Establishing Your "Why"

Before you dive into building websites, picking out color palettes, or obsessing over which photo filter makes your morning coffee look the most "authentic," you've got to get to the root of it all: your why.

Your why is the heartbeat of your brand. It's the reason your business exists, the spark that got you started, and the thing that keeps you moving even on days when the inbox is overflowing and your to-do list looks like a CVS receipt. It's what gives meaning to your marketing, purpose to your positioning, and consistency to your content.

Without a clear why, your brand becomes a Frankenstein's monster of disconnected tactics. One moment you're playful, the next you're polished, then you're trying to mimic that other brand you saw on TikTok that's crushing it. It's chaos. And chaos doesn't convert.

Let's dig in. Let's get personal. And let's get honest about what really drives your business.

Why Finding Your Why Isn't Fluff (Even If It Sounds Like It)

You've probably heard it before. From TED Talks to self-help books, everyone seems obsessed with the idea of purpose. And honestly? That's because it matters.

Your why is your brand's magnetic north. It's the belief system at the center of everything you do. When it's clear, it shows. Your message becomes more than a pitch-it becomes a story. A movement. A vibe.

People don't just buy *what* you do. They buy *why* you do it. Especially in the digital world, where consumers are bombarded with choices and algorithms are designed to surface brands that feel "real," a strong why is what makes people pause, pay attention, and lean in.

A business with a defined why doesn't just sell products or services-it sells a perspective. A mission. A promise. That emotional connection is what turns one-time buyers into loyal fans.

The 3-Layer Why Framework

Let's break this down into something tangible. Your "why" isn't just one big idea-it has layers, each tied to a different part of your brand's identity. Together, they make your message deeper, richer, and way more relatable. Think of it like a three-part harmony: each voice is distinct, but when combined, they create a fuller sound.

1. Your Personal Why

Start with the most intimate part of your brand-you. Why are you here, doing *this* work, and not something else entirely? What is it about this business or mission that keeps you going when everything feels overwhelming?

Your personal why is the emotional fuel behind your business. It's not always about a big "aha" moment. Sometimes it's a slow burn-a realization that this work simply matters to you in a way nothing else does. Maybe it's born out of your own experience, a pain you once had to overcome, or a need you saw go unmet for too long.

Think about the story behind the story. What was happening in your life before this idea started taking shape? Was there a moment of frustration? A deep desire for change? A personal breakthrough? That's where the roots are.

For example, a nutrition coach's personal why might stem from years of struggling with food guilt and body image. They're not just selling meal plans-they're helping others rewrite a narrative they know all too well. Or a web designer might remember watching their parent's small business struggle to compete online, and now they've made it their mission to help small businesses stand out in a digital world.

This part of your why connects to emotion. And emotion creates resonance. It gives your brand texture, vulnerability, and humanity. When your audience hears *why you care*, they start to care too.

The key here is honesty. Your personal why doesn't need to be overly polished or performative. It just needs to be *real*. It's okay if it's still evolving. It's okay if it's imperfect. You're human-and people relate to that.

2. Your Customer Why

Now let's shift focus. Step outside your own head for a second and ask, "Why does this matter to them?"

Your customer why is where empathy meets strategy. It's about understanding your ideal customer's world-what they're struggling with, what they dream about, what gets in their way, and how your work fits into their story.

This is where a lot of brands go wrong. They focus too much on features and not enough on outcomes. They talk about what their product does but forget to explain why it matters. And in a world where attention spans are short and competition is fierce, relevance is everything.

To define your customer why, put yourself in their shoes. What's frustrating them? What do they wish someone would just *get*? What feels overwhelming or impossible? What do they want to change?

Let's say you're a business coach. Your customer isn't just looking for spreadsheets and sales funnels. They want clarity. They want confidence. They want to stop spinning their wheels and start seeing progress. If you're a yoga instructor, your students aren't just after flexibility-they want peace of mind, relief from stress, a moment of calm in a chaotic week.

By aligning your story with theirs, you create connection. And connection is the first step to conversion.

This layer is about showing your audience that you *see* them. That you've thought about their needs. That you've built your solution with them in mind. When people feel understood, they start to trust-and trust is the foundation of any long-term relationship.

3. Your Business Why

Now take another step back. Zoom out and look at the big picture. What kind of impact do you want your business to have beyond individual transactions? What's the greater purpose that fuels your growth?

Your business why is the vision piece. It's the part that says, "We're not just here to make money-we're here to make a difference." That doesn't mean you have to be a nonprofit or a world-changing enterprise. But it does mean thinking beyond just revenue.

Maybe you're here to change how your industry does business. Maybe you're here to offer an alternative to something that feels broken. Maybe you're here to create access, build community, or flip a narrative that's held people back for too long.

A personal trainer's business why might be about redefining what fitness looks like-moving away from shame-based marketing and toward body positivity and strength for every shape and size. A copywriter's business why might be about helping ethical brands communicate with clarity so they can compete with louder, less scrupulous competitors.

This is your mission. Your reason for scaling. Your guiding light when it's time to hire, expand, or pivot. The business why helps keep your decisions in alignment. It helps you say yes to the right things-and no to the ones that just look good on paper.

Layering It All Together

Here's how these three whys work in harmony:

Let's say you own a small scale gym.

- **Personal why**: You've seen firsthand how fitness changes lives and you want to help others feel strong, confident, and capable.
- **Customer why**: You serve busy parents who feel left behind by traditional gyms. You provide accessible, flexible programs that meet them where they are.
- **Business why**: You want to create a community-driven space that challenges toxic fitness culture and empowers people to move their bodies with joy and purpose.

All three layers feed each other. Together, they form the foundation of a brand that's emotionally compelling, strategically smart, and built for long-term growth.

When you define your three-layer why, you unlock more than just a good elevator pitch. You unlock clarity. Consistency. Confidence. And that shows up everywhere-from your website copy to your Instagram captions to how you talk about your work in person.

These aren't just brand exercises. They're alignment tools. And when your brand is aligned, people notice-and respond.

Finding the Words That Actually Fit

Once you've done some soul-searching, the next step is putting your why into language that feels natural. Not corporate. Not "agency speak." But words that sound like *you*.

Ask yourself:

- What do I believe about the work I do?
- What do I wish more people understood about this industry?
- What change am I trying to make in someone's life?
- What gets me fired up (in a good or bad way)?
- What kind of impact makes me proud?

Jot down answers. Don't overthink it. This is brainstorming, not branding (yet). Look for themes. Patterns. Phrases that feel honest.

Then start shaping your why statement.

Here's a fill-in-the-blank to kick things off:

> *"I/We believe that [core belief]. That's why I/we [what you do], so that [impact you want to have]."*

Try a few versions. Read them out loud. Share them with a trusted peer. If it feels stiff or fake, rework it until it clicks.

Example: *"We believe wellness should feel human, not high-pressure. That's why we offer personalized coaching and real talk-so people can feel good without feeling overwhelmed."*

The goal is a statement you can stand behind-not something that belongs in a pitch deck.

How Your Why Shows Up in Your Digital DNA

Now here's where it gets exciting. Your why isn't just a mission statement that lives on your About page or collects digital dust at the bottom of a brand deck. It's the thread that runs through every touchpoint of your online presence. It's a filter that helps you make decisions. A compass that points you in the right direction. A tone-setter that gives your brand its personality.

Let's start with your messaging. Your why becomes the undercurrent of your copywriting. Whether it's your homepage headline, your Instagram bio, or the CTA at the bottom of your newsletter, your words should sound like someone who knows what they stand for. A strong why brings consistency and confidence to your voice. You stop writing to "everyone" and start speaking directly to *your* people. The ones who see your message and think, "Finally, someone gets it."

It also shows up in your visual identity. That's right-your why even shapes how things *look*. If your core belief is about creativity and freedom, you're probably not rocking a black-and-white site with Times New Roman fonts. You're likely using vibrant colors, playful typefaces, maybe even custom illustrations. If your why is about helping people simplify, your site might be clean, minimal, and calming. Your imagery might use lots of whitespace. The experience of *seeing* your site should reflect the *feeling* you want to create.

Your why also steers the kind of stories you tell. Every post, reel, tweet, or video is a chance to reinforce your mission. When you share a customer win, a behind-the-scenes moment, or even a hard lesson learned, your why should be the thread tying it all together. That's what makes storytelling authentic-not just what you say, but why you're saying it.

And let's not forget testimonials and social proof. The kinds of reviews you highlight (and even the way you ask for them) can reflect your why. If you believe in empowerment, you might feature client stories that show personal growth. If you stand for transparency, you might spotlight feedback that praises your honesty and integrity-even the stuff that includes a little constructive criticism. It's not just about praise-it's about alignment.

Even your SEO strategy can align with your why. Think about the keywords you target. If your mission is to educate and empower, you'll naturally lean into content that answers questions, breaks down myths, or offers clear how-tos. You won't just be chasing clicks-you'll be building trust.

When your why drives your creative choices, your brand stops feeling like a collection of tactics and starts becoming an experience. Your website doesn't just "work"-it *feels* like you. Your content doesn't just attract views-it sparks connection. Your brand doesn't just exist-it lives, breathes, and leaves an impression.

People can sense when a brand is aligned. It feels intentional. Authentic. Trustworthy. And in a crowded digital world, that feeling is everything.

Why-Gone-Wrong & And How It Got Fixed

Let me tell you about one of the most satisfying transformations I've ever seen-a local restaurant that had all the ingredients for success but none of the soul.

This was an established business in the heart of a busy area. For years, it had been the kind of place people went out of habit. But under the previous owner, it lost its spark. The service was inconsistent. The food was forgettable. And most importantly, the purpose behind it had vanished. Eventually, the business hit a wall. It stopped being a place people were excited to visit-and became a cautionary tale.

Then came the new owners. A young couple with hospitality backgrounds and a passion for revitalizing community spaces. They weren't just buying a restaurant-they were buying into the belief that food connects people, and that every neighborhood deserves a place that feels like home.

They did the big things right: remodeled the space, revamped the menu, hired staff who actually cared. But digitally? It was still a mess.

The website was sleek. Beautiful photos, modern fonts, even some clever animations. But conversions? Crickets. Reservations were slow. Online orders were almost non-existent. Engagement on social media was flat.

Why? Because the messaging was hollow. It was like reading a menu designed by a branding agency that had never stepped foot in the restaurant. It used all the "right" words-but none of the *real* ones. There was no cohesion. No voice. No soul. Definitely no why.

We hit pause and sat down with the new owners. We asked the same question we always do: "Why did you take this on?"

And their answer stopped us in our tracks. They wanted to create a space where people could reconnect-over food, over laughter, over moments that didn't involve screens. They believed in slow evenings with great drinks, in meals that reminded people why they vacationed there, in a restaurant that was more than just a place to eat.

They wanted to bring purpose back into the space. To rebuild trust with locals. To take something forgotten and make it feel alive again.

None of that was coming through in their branding.

So we rewrote everything-from the tagline to the menu descriptions to the About page. We dropped the generic foodie buzzwords and focused on their values: comfort, connection, community. We told their story, not just their offerings. We shared photos of the new owners behind the counter. Notes from returning customers who remembered what the place *used to be*, and were amazed by what it had become.

We also tweaked the visuals. Warmer colors. Custom graphics and photography. More people, fewer flat lays. Less polish, more personality.

Within months, reservations increased. Repeat customers became vocal advocates. Their Instagram post comments were full of people sharing memories of the spot-and thanking the owners for bringing it back to life.

The turning point? Their why finally had a voice.

It wasn't about being trendy or perfect. It was about being real. About reconnecting the brand to the heart that fueled it.

That's the power of a clearly defined why. It doesn't just improve your messaging-it brings your brand *back to life*.

What Happens When You Nail Your Why

When you truly lock in your why, your brand starts to breathe. You:

- Make faster, clearer decisions
- Know what content fits (and what doesn't)
- Attract aligned customers or collaborators
- Stop comparing yourself to competitors
- Feel more confident about how you show up online

Even better? You stop second-guessing every little detail. Because when your purpose is clear, your path is clearer too.

Exercise: Revisit Your Initial Why Statement

At the beginning of this chapter we asked you to craft your initial why statement. Now after reading the previous pages, and doing some soul searching lets revisit this together. Fill in this sentence with any adjustments:

> *"I/We believe that [core belief]. That's why I/we [what you do], so that [impact you want to have]."*

Try at least three versions. Don't worry about being perfect-just honest. Play with the language until it feels right. When you hit the version that makes you nod and say, "Yes. That's me," you've found it.

Write it down. Post it somewhere visible. Revisit it often.

Because your why isn't just the starting point of your digital brand-it's the fuel that keeps it going.

Next up, we'll start turning that fuel into fire by identifying your audience.

Chapter 3

Identifying Your Targets

So, you've unearthed your "why." Great job-you've just built your internal compass. Now it's time to aim it. Because having a purpose without knowing *who* it's for is like throwing darts in the dark. You might hit something, but it won't be what you intended.

Let's make one thing clear: not everyone is your audience. And that's a *good* thing. The tighter you define your targets, the stronger your messaging becomes, the easier your design decisions get, and the more magnetic your Digital DNA becomes. Let's break down how to find your people-and build a digital presence they actually care about.

Who Are You Really Talking To?

Too often, brands try to appeal to everyone and end up resonating with no one. When you try to be everything to everybody, you water down your voice until it sounds like corporate oatmeal. Bland, beige, and forgettable.

So let's put a stake in the ground.

You need to know:

- Who they are
- What they want
- Where they hang out
- What drives their decisions
- What frustrates them
- What excites them

Sound like a tall order? Don't worry-we're about to walk through it step by step.

Create Your Audience Personas (Without the Buzzword Nonsense)

Let's keep it real. Audience personas don't have to be long-winded fiction. You don't need to name your ideal customer "Wendy, a 32-year-old dog mom from

Panama City who drinks coffee and listens to true crime podcasts." Unless Wendy is *really* your target, of course.

Instead, focus on patterns and motivations:

- Demographics: Age range, location, job title, income level.
- Psychographics: Pain points, goals, habits, values.
- Behaviors: Where they consume content, what platforms they use, how they research.

You're not trying to get creepy-you're trying to understand what makes them tick so you can meet them where they are, in a way that feels authentic.

Use Real Data, Not Just Gut Feelings

Yes, intuition is helpful-but let's mix in some facts:

- **Google Analytics** – Check audience breakdowns by age, location, interests.
- **Social Insights** – Facebook, Instagram, and LinkedIn all offer audience analytics.
- **Customer Interviews** – You'd be surprised how much people will tell you when you just ask.

- **CRM & Email Data** – Review click-throughs, open rates, and user paths.

Pro tip: don't assume. Verify. "We think our clients are mostly 40-something CEOs" is a *very* different statement than "80% of our traffic is from women ages 25–34 on mobile."

Target the Problem, Not the Person

It is very easy to talk "at" people. However we want to talk "with" prospective clients. In order to do this, you need to understand what your customers are looking for and address their pain points, not just share who and what you do. Here's where it gets fun-and a bit philosophical. People don't always know what they need. But they always *feel* their problems.

That's why you should aim for problems and outcomes instead of just labels:

- Don't sell guided tours.

  Sell "getting the insider version of the city while everyone else follows the map."
- Don't sell hotel bookings.

  Sell "waking up steps from the beach without spending hours on TripAdvisor."
- Don't sell travel insurance.

  Sell "peace of mind when flights get weird and luggage goes rogue."
- Don't sell destination marketing.

  Sell "putting your town on the map-literally."

When you frame things around problems and desires, people feel seen-and your message becomes instantly more powerful.

Segment Like a Pro

You don't have to have *one* audience. In fact, most brands serve multiple types of people. What matters is that you tailor your communication accordingly.

Try segmenting your targets into tiers or clusters.

Primary Audience – Your Bread-and-Butter

This is your main squeeze. The people you built the business for. They're the ones who pay the bills, drive the majority of your revenue, and align perfectly with your offers. When you write content, design your website, or plan a campaign, this is the group you have in mind first.

Your primary audience should feel like your brand is speaking *directly* to them. They see your messaging and think, "Yes. That's me." They've got the problem you solve, the budget to solve it, and they're actively looking for the kind of solution you provide. If you're a plastic surgeon, your primary audience might be adults in their 30s–50s seeking cosmetic procedures. If you're a tour operator on 30A, it might be families planning summer vacations or retirees looking for an easy adventure. Bottom line: these are your people.

Secondary Audience – The Decision Influencers

They might not be the ones swiping the credit card, but they absolutely help decide *who* does. Think: executive assistants who research vendors, adult children helping a parent book a specialist, or partners nudging the final vacation choice. These folks play the behind-the-scenes role of researcher, validator, or trusted advisor.

If your messaging doesn't at least *nod* to them, you risk getting screened out early. The secondary audience often finds your content first-and they're the ones passing the link along. Make sure your messaging gives them the confidence to say, "Hey, you should check this out." That means clarity, credibility, and reassurance baked into every piece of content.

Tertiary Audience – The Long Game

This is your peripheral orbit-people who might buy from you later, refer others, or collaborate with you in the future. Think interns who will one day be decision-makers, neighboring businesses who could become partners, or a loyal blog reader who isn't a customer now but shares your stuff regularly.

These folks may not seem important today, but they help build your brand ecosystem. They amplify your voice, offer unexpected opportunities, and help keep your community warm. Tertiary audiences are why you maintain a presence on social media, nurture your email list, or keep blogging-even when it doesn't always lead to instant leads.

Create messaging that speaks to each one differently. They don't need the same email, the same landing page, or the same tone. Customize it.

Your Targets Shape Your Entire Ecosystem

When you truly understand who your audience is, it transforms everything:

- **Website Design**: Fonts, layouts, navigation structure-all of it should match their preferences.
- **Tone of Voice:** Speak how they speak. Casual? Buttoned up? Energetic? Thoughtful?
- **Platform Choices:** Are they on LinkedIn, YouTube, Reddit? Don't chase platforms-chase *presence*.
- **Lead Magnets & CTAs:** What's actually useful to them? What do they *want* to download?
- **Ad Messaging:** No more generic taglines. Write to their needs and mindset.

Exercise: Define 2 Core Personas

Try filling in this mini-profile for each of your two core audiences:

- **Name (internal):** Short, memorable label (e.g. "Busy Brenda").
- **Age Range:** Typical age span (e.g. 30–45).
- **Role:** Job title or decision-making role.
- **Pain Point:** Main challenge they need solved.
- **Goal:** What they want to achieve.
- **Platforms:** Where they spend time online.
- **Buying Behavior:** How they make decisions.
- **Content Style:** What kind of content they prefer.

Write them down. Revisit often. Refine. These aren't permanent-they're evolving. But they will keep you grounded in who you're actually building your Digital DNA for.

Chapter 4

Constructing Your DNA (Digital Ecosystem)

Welcome to the construction site-don't worry, you won't need steel-toe boots. In this chapter, we're diving into the details of actually building your digital ecosystem. If your why is the heart and your audience is the brain, your ecosystem is the skeleton, skin, and nervous system. It's the stuff people interact with every day-and how they form opinions about your brand.

A digital ecosystem is the full collection of online tools, platforms, and touchpoints you use to present your brand and engage your audience. It includes your website, social media platforms, email campaigns, directories, CRMs, analytics, landing pages, review sites, scheduling tools, e-commerce plugins, and more. But here's the thing-it's not just about being present on all these platforms. It's about being intentional, connected, and cohesive.

Take Inventory: Know What You've Got

Let's begin by mapping what you already have in place. Most people are surprised at the gaps that pop up when they do a proper audit. Maybe your Instagram is on point, but your website is still running on a theme from 2012. Or you've got great blog content, but no SEO structure behind it. Or you're killing it on TikTok but haven't claimed your Google Business profile.

Document everything-from your software tools to your public-facing channels. Where does your brand currently exist online? Where are you actively publishing content? Where are you passively listed but not paying attention?

This snapshot becomes your foundation. It's like a blueprint. You can't build anything if you don't know what's already nailed down, half-built, or missing entirely.

Assign Purpose to Every Piece

Once you've mapped your assets, ask: What role does each piece play? Your website isn't just there to "have a website." It's your digital HQ. It should load quickly, reflect your brand voice, guide users effortlessly, and drive conversions. It should educate, build trust, and inspire action-all without requiring a map to navigate.

Your social media channels? Not a popularity contest. It's not about followers-it's about building community, starting conversations, and leading people back to your home base.

Every platform, every piece of content, every button-should serve a purpose. If it doesn't? Either clarify the role or cut it.

Your Website: Your Digital Home Base

Let's talk about that home base: your website. It's not a digital business card; it's a conversion machine. It should feel like walking into your storefront-warm, clear, and unmistakably you.

Start with speed. Nothing kills trust like a slow site. Then focus on structure. Is your navigation simple? Is your content skimmable? Is your CTA easy to find (and not buried under three carousels and a wall of buzzwords)?

Your site should also be:

- Mobile-friendly
- Voice-aligned
- Built for next steps

We will touch more deeply on these items in a later chapter but remember: design isn't just about pretty colors. It's about guiding behavior.

The Strands: Connect the Dots

Around your website are what I call the "strands"-social media platforms, business directories, review sites, and third-party listings. These are the outer layers of your ecosystem. They should orbit your brand, all singing from the same song sheet.

Your Instagram bio, LinkedIn headline, Yelp description, and Google Business profile should all echo your core message. Not word-for-word, but close enough that if someone hops between platforms, they know they're still looking at *you*.

Strands are powerful because they multiply your exposure-but only if they're consistent. Think of them like satellites transmitting your brand signal. If some are fuzzy or off-brand, you're diluting your reach.

Systems + Automation: Let It Flow

Of course, having all these parts is only half the battle. You need systems to connect them. Automation is your best friend here. It's the connective tissue of your digital body.

Let's say someone fills out a form on your website. Where does their info go? Into a spreadsheet you'll never open again? Or into a CRM where they're tagged, tracked, and entered into a welcome sequence? Done right, automation turns casual interest into sustained engagement. You can:

- Trigger follow-up emails
- Send calendar invites
- Deliver lead magnets instantly
- Nurture leads with pre-written sequences

You're not replacing human interaction-you're scaling it.

Monitor What Matters: Metrics + Maintenance

Now let's talk about your dashboard. If you're not measuring, you're guessing. And digital marketing is no place for guesswork.

Use tools like Analytics, Heat mapping tools, social media insights, and email dashboards to track performance. Pay attention to:

- Bounce rates (where are people leaving?)
- Click-through rates (what's grabbing attention?)
- Conversion rates (what's turning interest into action?)

Pick 3–5 KPIs that align with your business goals and track them regularly. You don't need a spreadsheet from hell. You just need clear, actionable data.

Don't Fall Into These Traps

Let's hit a few common mistakes:

1. **Shiny Object Syndrome:** It's tempting to chase every new tool or trend. Resist the urge. If it doesn't support your mission, it's just noise.
2. **Overbuilding:** More platforms ≠ more value. Focus on the ones that serve your audience best.
3. **Inconsistency:** If your tone shifts wildly between platforms, people get confused. Stay true to your voice.
4. **Data Overload:** Track what matters, ignore the rest. Your goal is clarity, not chaos.
5. **Lack of Follow-Up:** Capturing leads is step one. Following up is where the magic happens. Don't drop the ball here.

Build to Scale

Your ecosystem should support not only where you are now-but where you're headed. As your business grows, your digital infrastructure needs to keep up.

Can your email platform handle more subscribers? Can your CMS support multiple landing pages, product updates, or new services? Is your site optimized for increased traffic? Are your automations scalable?

Don't build for today's version of you. Build for the version that's coming.

Your digital ecosystem doesn't need to be flashy. It needs to *function*. It needs to work together, talk to each other, and serve a larger goal. When it does, something clicks. Your brand starts to hum. People notice. And your Digital DNA? It goes from "present" to "powerful."

Chapter 5

Building Your Brand

Let's talk about your brand. Not your logo. Not your color palette. Not even your tagline. Your *brand*. The thing people remember about you when you're not in the room. The feeling your name evokes. The vibe your content gives off before they've even read the first sentence.

In a digital world overflowing with content and competitors, your brand is the thing that cuts through the noise. It's what makes someone pause mid-scroll. What makes someone choose *you* over a dozen near-identical options. And building a brand doesn't happen overnight. It's not something you buy-it's something you craft, shape, and grow over time with care, consistency, and a strong sense of who you are.

So let's build your brand. With intention. With personality. And without a single whiff of generic corporate jargon.

What a Brand *Really* Is

A brand isn't just your logo or your font choices. It's your promise. Your reputation. It's the impression people carry after experiencing you-whether that experience happened on your website, in a DM, through a customer review, or face-to-face.

You don't get to declare what your brand is. People decide for you-based on how you show up. Which means: your brand is being shaped every day, whether you're being intentional about it or not. From the tone of your email responses to the packaging of your product to the way you reply to a bad review-it all speaks.

So, the question becomes: are you shaping your brand, or letting it happen by accident?

Start with Personality, Not Pretty Things

Most people start branding with the visuals. But let's rewind. Before you touch a color swatch or fiddle with your fonts, you need to know your brand *personality*.

That's your voice. Your attitude. The energy you bring to the room-digital or otherwise.

Are you bold and cheeky? Calm and supportive? Polished and professional? Your personality sets the tone for how you write, how you speak, how you market-and ultimately, how people experience you.

Once you know your vibe, it becomes your filter. If something doesn't sound or feel like your brand, it doesn't go out. Full stop.

One way to ground this is to choose a few core personality traits-words like honest, clever, empathetic, disruptive, or empowering-and let those guide the way you speak, create, and show up.

Dressing the Part: Your Visual Identity

Okay, now we can talk about looks. Your visual identity is your brand's outfit-the stuff people see first. It includes your logo, your colors, your typography, your photos and illustrations, and the general aesthetic of your content.

But here's the kicker: good design isn't about being trendy. It's about being consistent and aligned. Everything should *look* like it came from the same brand, whether it's a social post, a landing page, or your invoice.

Pick a primary and secondary color palette and use them consistently. Choose two or three fonts max. Decide if your brand feels clean and minimal, bold and high-contrast, vintage and earthy-whatever it is, stick with it. People start to trust what they recognize. And consistency builds recognition.

Speak With Intention: Your Messaging

Branding is more than a visual vibe-it's also about *how* you talk. Messaging is where your personality and values meet your customer's reality. It's your elevator pitch. Your About page. The headline on your homepage. The voice in your captions.

Great messaging isn't about being clever-it's about being *clear*. It should feel natural, confident, and easy to connect with. Ditch the jargon and marketing fluff. Talk to your audience like a real person (remember the personas we built earlier?).

A handy formula to ground your message:

> "We help [who] do [what], so they can [outcome]."

Like: "We help overwhelmed business owners build digital brands that feel like them-so they can grow without burning out."

Simple. Effective. Memorable.

What You Stand For: Values and Mission

More and more, people want to buy from brands that stand for something. So what do you believe in? What do you fight for-or against? What drives you to do this work beyond just making a sale?

Your values and mission shouldn't just be words on a website footer. They should show up in your pricing, your partnerships, your hiring practices, your content, your offers. They should inform *how* you show up-not just what you sell.

And no, you don't have to please everyone. Great brands take a stand. And people will either feel deeply connected-or respectfully walk away. Either way, you're building something authentic.

Your Brand Experience: More Than Just a Look

Here's the part a lot of brands overlook. Your brand isn't just what you say or how you look-it's how people *feel* when they interact with you. It's the micro-moments.

That confirmation email-was it warm or robotic? That DM reply-did it sound like a human or a customer service bot? That onboarding guide-was it clear, helpful, even a little delightful?

Every touchpoint is an opportunity to reinforce your brand. The tone of your contact form, the design of your invoice, even your out-of-office reply-it all contributes to the experience. Make it thoughtful.

The Trust Factor

A strong brand isn't about shouting "Trust me!"–it's about behaving in a way that earns trust.

That means showing up consistently. Owning your mistakes. Providing real value before asking for anything in return. Sharing client results, reviews, or behind-the-scenes content that shows you're the real deal.

Trust is a long game. But it's THE game worth playing.

The Real-World Gut Check

Picture your brand as a person walking into a networking event. How do they carry themselves? Are they warm and welcoming? Buttoned-up and all-business? Do they crack a joke, ask questions, inspire confidence?

Now compare that vibe to your digital touchpoints-your website, your social feed, your emails. Do they match the energy? Or does it feel like a brand with an identity crisis?

Great branding isn't about being the loudest or slickest in the room. It's about feeling genuine. And being consistent enough that people start to trust you-even if they've never met you.

Your Brand Is a Living Thing

You don't just "finish" your brand and never touch it again. Like any good relationship, it evolves. As you grow, your brand should grow too. Your visuals might need refreshing. Your message might need refining. Your values might become sharper.

Check in with your brand every 6–12 months. Does it still feel aligned? Does it still reflect who you are and who you serve? If not, it's time to recalibrate.

Chapter 6

Website

Here we are-the beating heart of your digital ecosystem: your website. This is where your brand, your voice, your visuals, and your strategy all come together in one central hub. It's not just where people "learn more"-it's where they decide if they trust you, like you, and want to work with you. And it all happens in a matter of seconds.

Your website is your digital handshake, your home base, your storefront. And whether someone's landing on it from a Google search, a social post, or a referral link, they're showing up with questions. If your site doesn't answer them quickly-and confidently-they're gone.

Let's walk through what it takes to create a site that works around the clock to connect, convert, and represent you well.

Your Website Is Not Just a Brochure

Too many websites are still stuck in brochure mode-overloaded with info, light on clarity, and designed to impress rather than connect. But people don't want to dig. They want quick answers. So your homepage needs to immediately answer the big four:

Who are you? What do you do? Why should they care? And what should they do next?

Think of your homepage like Grand Central Station. It doesn't need to be flashy-it needs to be helpful and dispatch visitors to the proper content quickly. When someone lands there, they should instantly know if they're in the right place and what they're supposed to do next.

Guide Them with Structure

A good website doesn't just look nice-it guides your visitor through a journey. Think of it like hosting a dinner party. First, you welcome them (homepage). Then you introduce yourself (about page). Then you show them the good stuff you offer (services/products). Next, you prove you're legit (testimonials or case studies). And finally, you invite them to take action (your call to action).

That flow should be easy to follow. Use clear headers, intuitive navigation, clean layouts, and natural next steps. Let visitors explore without getting lost or overwhelmed. Make the path from curiosity to conversion feel obvious.

Write Like a Human

In an evolving AI world, Copywriting can make or break your site. Design may draw people in, but it's the words that close the deal. Your copy should sound like you, speak to your ideal audience, and make them feel seen.

This isn't the place for jargon or trying to sound like every other business in your industry. It's a place to connect. Imagine explaining what you do to a smart friend over coffee. That's the voice you want.

Instead of saying "We provide comprehensive consulting solutions," say "We help you finally stop guessing and start growing." Instead of "Our services deliver optimized outcomes," say "We'll help you reach your goals-faster, easier, and with less stress."

Speak like a human. Write like you care.

Design for the Phone First (It's not 2012 anymore)

If your website isn't mobile-friendly, it might as well not exist. We're not living in the dial-up days anymore. People aren't waiting to get home to check out your site on a desktop. They're browsing while in line at the grocery store, on the couch during a Netflix binge, or in the passenger seat during a road trip. If your site can't keep up with how people actually live and browse today, you're losing them.

More than half of all web traffic happens on mobile devices-and in many industries, it's even higher. In fact, for local service providers, restaurants, e-commerce, and healthcare providers, mobile can account for 70% or more of total visits. That means your site's first impression isn't being made on a laptop-it's being made on a phone.

Mobile-first design isn't just about shrinking your site down to fit a smaller screen. It's about *rethinking* how your content, layout, and functionality work for touchscreens, short attention spans, and one-thumb navigation. That means:

- Big, easy-to-click buttons. No one wants to fat-finger their way through your menu.
- A clean, single-column layout that scrolls naturally and intuitively.
- Fonts that are readable without zooming in like a digital detective.
- Menus that are easy to open, use, and close-without frustration.
- Quick loading speeds-because no one's waiting more than a couple seconds for your homepage to appear.

And here's a pro tip that too many overlook: *test it*. Don't assume your mobile site works just because your platform says it's responsive. Actually open your site on an iPhone. On an Android. On a tablet. Rotate the screen. Tap the buttons. Go through your contact form. Check how your pop-ups behave. Be your own user.

If you find yourself squinting, pinching, or scrolling side to side-you've got work to do.

Mobile-first doesn't mean the desktop is dead. It means *start* with mobile and scale up, not the other way around. Prioritize what's essential. Make every word count. Make every click effortless.

Because when your site feels good on a phone, it feels good everywhere.

Use Visuals That Show, Not Just Decorate

Your visuals should tell your story-not just fill space. That means real images whenever possible. Show your face. Show your team. Show your work. People want to see the human side of your brand.

If you're using video, make it count. A quick, honest intro can go a long way in building trust. Keep it short, keep it engaging, and keep it relevant. Don't autoplay unless it adds value (and doesn't annoy people). And for the love of good design, skip the stiff stock photography. We've all seen that same smiling handshake photo a hundred times.

Make Your CTAs Count

Your Call to Action (CTA) is the moment of truth-the place where your visitor says "yes" or clicks away. Don't waste it. Every page on your site should have a clear, benefit-driven CTA.

Instead of "Contact Us," say "Let's talk about your project." Instead of "Learn More," try "See how we can help." Your CTA should feel like a natural next step, not a commitment to a sales pitch.

And don't be afraid to repeat it. People don't always scroll back up to find a button. Make it easy.

Keep Forms Friendly

Nobody likes filling out a form that feels like applying for a mortgage. Keep your forms short and simple. Ask for the essentials. You can always follow up with more questions later.

Also-add some personality. A friendly line like "We'll get back to you within a day, no robots involved" makes a big difference. It signals that a real person is on the other side, and that builds trust.

Basic SEO Isn't Optional

Let's clear something up: you don't need to be an SEO guru to make your website work for search engines-but you *do* need to understand the basics. Think of SEO (Search Engine Optimization) as the digital signage that helps people find your site in the chaos of the internet. You could have the best site in the world, but if no one sees it? It's like opening a beautiful restaurant in the middle of a forest with no roads.

SEO isn't about gaming Google anymore. It's about making your site readable, useful, and accessible-both to your audience and the search engines trying to deliver relevant results. When done right, SEO quietly does its job in the background, helping more of the right people find you at the right time.

Start with your content. Use natural, relevant keywords in your page titles, headings, and body text-but avoid stuffing. If you're a local yoga studio, don't say "yoga studio yoga classes yoga near me" ten times in one paragraph. Instead, work your core phrases in organically. Make it easy for both your readers and search engines to understand what you're about.

Next up: meta titles and descriptions. These are the little snippets that show up on Google's results page when your site appears in a search. If you don't write them, Google will pull whatever it wants from your page-and trust us, it's usually awkward. Take the time to write a unique meta title and description for each page. Use it to summarize what the page is about and why someone should click.

Your images also matter. Compress them so they load quickly-nobody likes a slow site. And make sure each image has alt text (alternative text), which not only improves accessibility for screen readers but also gives Google more context about your content.

Then there's your URLs. Keep them clean and descriptive. Instead of "yoursite.com/page?id=48392abc," try "yoursite.com/branding-strategy." This helps both search engines *and* humans understand what the page is about at a glance.

Also, don't sleep on internal linking. That means linking to other pages on your own site-like from your blog post to your services page. It keeps people engaged and helps Google understand your site structure.

And here's the golden rule: write for humans first. Google is getting better every day at mimicking human judgment. If your content is genuinely helpful, easy to read, and well-organized, it'll naturally rise in the ranks.

SEO might sound intimidating at first, but start with these fundamentals and you'll be in a stronger position than most. And once your foundation is solid, you can always layer in more advanced strategies down the line. For now, just focus on clarity, quality, and relevance-and let Google do the rest.

Let Others Brag for You

Trust is currency online-and one of the fastest ways to build it is through the words and experiences of others. You can tell people how great you are until you're blue in the face, but it'll never hit the same as a real person saying, "This changed everything for me."

Testimonials, reviews, and case studies act like digital word-of-mouth. They show that you're not just talking the talk-you're delivering results. But here's the thing: not all testimonials are created equal. A throwaway quote like "They were awesome!" might feel nice, but it doesn't tell future customers anything useful.

You want testimonials that tell a story. What was the problem? What did you do to help? What changed afterward? Bonus points if it includes concrete outcomes-like increased sales, improved efficiency, peace of mind, or saved time. Add in a name, a photo, and a title (with permission), and now that story has weight.

Visual proof matters too. Have you worked with recognizable brands? Show their logos (even in grayscale). Got a killer before-and-after photo set? Share it. Have client stats that show real impact? Build them into a mini case study. These elements serve as social proof-and they create a domino effect of credibility.

If you're just getting started and don't have dozens of testimonials yet, no problem. Ask early clients or collaborators for feedback. Even a short quote about how easy it was to work with you, how responsive you were, or how you solved a frustrating issue can build trust. And as you grow, keep collecting stories. Make it part of your process.

The goal is to create a chorus of voices echoing your value-so prospects don't just have to take *your* word for it. They'll see that real people, just like them, took the leap-and are glad they did.

Don't Just Launch-Maintain

Your website isn't a "set it and forget it" situation. It's not a digital brochure that gets printed once and left untouched for years. It's a living, breathing part of your brand-and like anything living, it needs regular care to stay healthy.

Websites age fast. Content gets outdated. Links break. Staff bios change. Services evolve. And if you're not actively keeping up, your site can start to misrepresent who you are and what you offer. What was once a sleek, modern online home can quickly start to feel like walking into a store where the lights are flickering and the signage is from 2018.

Maintenance doesn't mean a full rebrand every quarter. It just means staying on top of the basics. Update your copy to reflect your current offerings. Refresh testimonials and case studies to include your most recent (and relevant) wins. Replace outdated headshots or photography with visuals that better reflect who you are today.

Fix broken links. Review your contact forms to make sure they still work (yes, really-forms break more often than you'd think). Check your load speeds, especially after adding new media. And give your homepage some love-sometimes a new headline or fresh feature section is enough to breathe new life into it.

Consider setting a recurring reminder-once a quarter is a great place to start. Think of it like a digital oil change. These quick check ups can help you spot problems early and make minor tweaks before they turn into big issues.

And don't underestimate the impression an up-to-date site gives. A fresh, maintained site signals that your business is active, engaged, and paying attention. A stale one? That raises questions. Don't let your best marketing tool start to feel like an abandoned storefront.

Stay on top of your site, and it will keep working for you-day in, day out.

Use Your Data

You don't have to be knee-deep in spreadsheets or speak fluent analytics to get value from your website data. But if you're flying completely blind, you're guessing-and guessing is expensive. Your website holds valuable insights about what's working and what's not, and all you have to do is check in and listen.

Start with the basics. Tools like Analytics, Heat maps, or even your website platform's built-in analytics can show you:

- Where visitors are coming from (Google search, Instagram, email, etc.)
- What pages they're landing on first
- How long they're staying on each page
- What they're clicking-or *not* clicking
- Where they're exiting or bouncing
- Which calls to action are getting clicks (and which ones aren't)

This kind of data tells a story. If people are landing on your homepage but leaving before clicking anywhere else, maybe your message isn't clear. If your most popular blog post gets tons of traffic but no conversions, maybe you need a stronger call to action on that page. If a specific service page has a high bounce rate, maybe the copy needs refining-or the offer needs repositioning.

Even small insights-like which headline variation gets more clicks or which image gets more scroll time-can guide smarter decisions. And you don't have to act on everything at once. Use the data to spot patterns and prioritize your fixes.

If you really want to get into the nitty-gritty, tools like Hotjar can even show you heatmaps (where users are hovering and clicking), screen recordings, and drop-off points in forms. It's like watching over your users' shoulders as they explore your site. It can be a little creepy-but also incredibly valuable.

Here's the point: your website is constantly giving you feedback. It's showing you what resonates, what confuses people, and where opportunities are hiding. Don't ignore it. Check in regularly-monthly is great, quarterly is a must-and use what you learn to improve user experience, increase conversions, and get more value out of every visitor.

Because great websites aren't just launched-they're optimized, refined, and evolved over time. Let your data lead the way.

Your website isn't just a digital placeholder. It's your first impression, your best salesperson, and your most reliable lead generator-if it's built right.

Make it honest. Make it helpful. Make it reflect the brand you're building everywhere else.

When done well, your website works for you while you sleep, sip coffee, or plan your next big move. It's not just a page-it's your platform for growth.

Chapter 7

Social Media

Social media is more than just posting a pic and slapping on a hashtag. It's a dynamic tool for building community, amplifying your message, driving traffic, and, yes-closing sales. But the trick is doing it *intentionally*, *consistently*, and with a tone that doesn't sound like you copied it from a motivational poster in someone's dentist office.

This chapter is your go-to guide for making social media work as a strategic, authentic, and dare I say, *enjoyable* part of your Digital DNA. Let's dive in, memes and all.

Choose Your Platforms With Purpose

You don't need to be on every social platform. Seriously, you don't get bonus points for burnout. What you *do* need is a consistent, intentional presence on the platforms that actually matter to your audience.

If you're selling to B2B decision-makers, LinkedIn is probably your playground. Selling lifestyle products? Instagram or TikTok might be your sweet spot. Sharing tutorials or commentary? YouTube is likely your best bet.

Here's how to figure out where you belong:

- **Where are my ideal customers already scrolling?** Think about where your audience naturally spends their time. Are they reading articles on LinkedIn during their coffee break? Watching DIY tutorials on YouTube? Binging TikToks late at night? Don't try to lure them somewhere new-go where they already are.

- **Which platforms actually match my brand's vibe?** Your tone and style matter. If your brand is polished and professional, LinkedIn or YouTube might make the most sense. If you're casual, cheeky, or visually-driven, Instagram or TikTok could be your jam. The goal is to feel like you belong in the feed-not like you accidentally wandered into the wrong party.

- What kind of content can I *actually* make-consistently and well?
  Be real with yourself here. If you hate being on camera, launching a YouTube channel might not be the best idea (yet). If writing's your thing, maybe you shine in newsletters or LinkedIn posts. Choose platforms where your content strengths and resources align, not ones that demand skills you dread.

Start small. One or two platforms, max. Show up, stay consistent, and get good. Once you've got momentum and a clear rhythm, then (and only then) consider branching out.

Because dominating one space beats blending into the background on five. Every time.

Define Your Voice and Vibe

Your social media voice is basically your brand's personality with a mic-and it's live, unscripted, and happening in real-time. It's the tone, attitude, and energy you bring to every post, comment, story, or reply. Are you witty and cheeky, throwing in a little sass with your strategy? Or maybe you're thoughtful and empowering, the kind of voice that feels like a supportive coach or trusted friend. Maybe you're all about cutting through the fluff-straightforward, no-nonsense, and refreshingly real. Whatever your vibe is, the key is to own it-and stick with it.

This voice becomes your signature. Even if someone covers your logo, your followers should still be able to say, "Oh yeah, this post *has* to be from them." That kind of brand recognition isn't built with fonts and colors alone-it's built with tone, consistency, and personality.

A helpful way to think about it: if your brand showed up at a party, what kind of guest would it be? Would people say, "They're hilarious and always have the best one-liners," or "They're super insightful, I always learn something from them," or even "They're the kind of person who just *gets* me"? That five-minute first impression? That's your social voice in action.

And your tone doesn't just live in your posts. It's everywhere:

- In how you write your captions-whether you use emojis, sentence fragments, or storytelling
- In how you respond to comments-are you casual, warm, playful, or formal?
- In your DMs-do you reply like a human or a call center?
- Even in your typos (own them-people love knowing there's a real person behind the screen)

Whatever you do, keep it human. Show behind-the-scenes moments. Let people in on your thought process. Don't be afraid to have an opinion (just maybe not *every* opinion). The internet is full of polished, perfect, and frankly boring content. But personality? That stands out. That gets remembered. And that's how you build connection-not just attention.

Because here's the truth: people don't connect with brands on social media. They connect with *people behind* the brands. So let yours show up loud and clear.

Create a Content Strategy (Yes, You Need One)

Let's face it, posting just to "stay active" is like walking into a room and saying, "I have nothing to say, but I didn't want to miss the party." Not exactly memorable. A content strategy, on the other hand, helps you show up with purpose. It's your plan for saying something meaningful every time you post-whether it's to inform, entertain, or inspire action.

To make things manageable, start thinking in content "buckets." These are categories that help you balance variety while staying aligned with your brand and goals. Here's how that breaks down:

Educate – This is your teacher hat. Share tips, explain concepts, or provide quick how-tos that make your audience feel smarter. When you demystify something complicated or offer a helpful checklist, you become a trusted resource-and that trust leads to clicks, follows, and eventually, conversions.

Entertain – Yes, you're allowed to have fun. Entertainment doesn't mean becoming a comedian (unless that's your brand), but it does mean sharing content that makes people laugh, nod, or feel something. That relatable meme about work-from-home life? That silly TikTok you made about industry jargon? These moments make your brand human.

Engage – Conversation is the currency of social media. Engagement content is designed to invite a response. Ask questions. Create polls. Encourage your audience to share their opinion or story. Whether it's "This or That" posts or "Caption This" challenges, make your followers feel like their voice matters.

Promote – This is the sales shelf in your digital store. Talk about your services, share your offers, or announce launches-but do it with clarity and confidence. Tell people what you're offering, why it's valuable, and how to get it. Don't shy away from selling-just balance it with value-driven content.

Proof – Time to show receipts. Share testimonials from happy clients, highlight successful case studies, or post reviews that make you proud. Nothing builds trust like real people saying, "This worked for me." Sprinkle in this social proof regularly to reinforce that your product or service delivers.

Every post should have a job to do. Maybe it drives traffic to your website, encourages comments, or boosts visibility. Whatever the goal, be intentional. Mix up your formats-stories, reels, carousels, static images, live videos-but keep the messaging consistent. Consistency doesn't mean boring-it means on-brand, every time.

A great content strategy doesn't just keep you organized-it gives you momentum. It transforms social media from a chore into a powerful extension of your brand's voice. So go ahead and plan like a pro. Your future self (and your audience) will thank you.

Planning Beats Posting On the Fly

One of the best-kept secrets of stress-free social media is planning. Winging it may feel spontaneous and artsy, but it's also the fastest route to inconsistency-and burnout. Planning your content in advance gives you structure, clarity, and yes, the freedom to actually be creative *without* scrambling for something to post at 10:43 p.m.

Start simple. Maybe it's a spreadsheet, a Trello board, or a Google Calendar. Maybe it's an actual printed planner you scribble in over coffee. Whatever your tool, the goal is to map out what you'll post, where it'll go, and what outcome you're aiming for. This could be weekly themes, monthly campaigns, or even daily post formats-whatever fits your flow.

Now enter the concept of batching. This is where you create several pieces of content in one sitting. Maybe you write three captions in an hour, film two videos in one afternoon, or design a week's worth of graphics on a rainy Saturday. Batching isn't just efficient-it helps you get into a creative rhythm so you're not switching mental gears every five minutes.

Once your content is ready, it's time to schedule. Tools like Buffer, Later, Meta Business Suite, Hootsuite, or even native platform schedulers allow you to queue your content in advance. You stay visible, even when life gets busy. Bonus: you'll stop feeling tethered to your phone like a social media hostage.

But planning doesn't mean you can't be spontaneous. When inspiration hits, you can still post in the moment. Planning just creates space for those moments-so they're not happening in a panic.

And here's the real magic: when you plan with intention, your content starts to align with everything else. Your launches. Your promotions. Your seasonal campaigns. Even your vacation schedule. You stop reacting and start orchestrating.

Bottom line: planning doesn't make your content robotic. It makes it *strategic*. And strategy, my friend, is how you show up online like a pro-without losing your mind in the process.

Engagement Isn't Optional-It's the Game

We have to get one thing straight: social media isn't a billboard. It's not just a place to dump content and peace out. It's a living, breathing conversation. And if you're not engaging, you're just that person at the party standing in the corner talking to themselves. Not a great look.

Yes, creating great content matters. But if you're not responding to comments, hopping into conversations, or acknowledging your followers-you're missing the magic. Engagement is where the connection happens. It's where your brand stops being a logo and starts becoming a *voice*.

Start small. When someone comments on your post, reply with more than just a heart emoji. Ask a follow-up question. Say thank you in a way that doesn't sound canned. If someone shares your post, go like their share and drop a comment. Show people you're paying attention-because attention is currency online.

Jump into threads that make sense for your brand. If you see a post in your niche where your expertise would be valuable, chime in. Not with a sales pitch-just a thoughtful, authentic take. It builds visibility, credibility, and sometimes even relationships that turn into collaborations or customers.

Don't just talk-listen. Use polls and questions to invite people into the conversation. Ask for their opinions, their experiences, their favorite tools, or their take on a trend. People love sharing when they feel like they're being heard. And when they do respond? Acknowledge it. Let them know you see them.

Here's the secret: engagement isn't about algorithms-it's about *humans*. And the more you show up as a real person (or a brand that acts like one), the more people will want to interact with you. Algorithms may reward engagement, but people *crave* it.

And this part's important: don't wait around hoping people will come to you. Go be the first to reach out. Compliment someone else's post. Drop a thoughtful comment on a peer's new video. DM someone who liked your post and say thanks. These little moments create momentum-and that's where the real growth starts.

So yes, a like is good. A comment is better. But a back-and-forth conversation? That's where your digital DNA stops being static and starts to *spark*. Social media isn't just about presence-it's about participation. Be someone worth talking to.

Metrics That Actually Matter

It's easy to get obsessed with vanity metrics-likes, follows, and shares. Watching likes roll in can feel like digital applause, and hey, who doesn't love a little validation? But if your goal is to build a business (not just a fan club), then it's time to stop obsessing over vanity metrics and start measuring what *actually* moves the needle.

Likes, views, and follower counts might give your ego a quick boost, but they don't pay the bills. Real impact comes from metrics that tie directly back to your goals-whether that's building awareness, driving traffic, converting leads, or growing your loyal customer base. So let's break it down.

- **Reach and Impressions (Awareness)**

  These numbers tell you how many eyeballs are seeing your content. Reach is the number of unique people who saw it; impressions count total views (including repeat ones). These are your baseline visibility stats. If your content isn't being seen, nothing else matters. But don't stop at reach-ask yourself *who* you're reaching, and whether they're the right people.

- **Engagement Rate (Interest)**

  This is where the magic begins. Are people liking, sharing, commenting, saving, or clicking on your content? Engagement shows that your audience isn't just scrolling-they're paying attention. It's a sign that your messaging is resonating and your tone is landing. A high engagement rate on a smaller audience is often more valuable than a huge following that stays silent.

- **Click-Through Rate (Traffic)**

  This one's the bridge between curiosity and action. Your click-through rate (CTR) tells you how many people actually *clicked* on a link in your post, story, or bio. It shows who you've intrigued enough to leave the platform and head to your site, your landing page, or your store. If you're posting strong CTAs but no one's clicking, it might be time to rework your copy or offer.

- Conversions (Leads/Sales)

This is the ultimate goal for many brands: turning attention into action. Conversions track how many people took the next step-whether that's filling out a form, booking a call, downloading a resource, or making a purchase. This is where your social media efforts start to show ROI. If the conversions aren't coming, but traffic is high, something may be off on your landing page or funnel.

- Follower Growth (Audience Building)

Sure, we said not to obsess over followers-but tracking how your audience grows (or shrinks) over time still matters. It's not about chasing big numbers; it's about understanding the quality and consistency of your audience. Are you attracting people who engage? Are they sticking around? Sudden drops or spikes can tell you a lot about what's working-or what's not.

Here's the key: track these metrics *over time*. Don't get hung up on one post bombing or one week being slow. Look for patterns. What content tends to perform best? What times of day get the most engagement? Which topics get people clicking or commenting? These insights will help you double down on what works–and cut the fluff.

Social media is part creativity, part data. So treat your metrics like feedback, not judgment. Use them to experiment, evolve, and sharpen your strategy. Because the goal isn't just to be seen–it's to be remembered, trusted, and acted upon.

Social Media Advertising: When to Pay to Play

Organic reach is valuable, but it has limits. You can create the world's most insightful, hilarious, perfectly timed post–but if the algorithm isn't feeling generous, it might not get the eyeballs it deserves. That's where social media advertising steps in. It's not about "cheating the system"–it's about amplifying what's already working so you can reach more of the *right* people, faster.

Think of ads like a megaphone. They don't replace your message-they help it carry further. Especially during key moments like launching a new product, promoting an event, or trying to build brand awareness in a new market, a small paid push can make a big difference.

But here's the thing: paid social works best when you're strategic. Don't just hit that little "Boost Post" button and hope for the best. Start with posts that have already proven themselves organically. If people are engaging with it on their own, chances are it'll do well when you put a few bucks behind it too.

Start small. You don't need a massive ad budget to see results. Even $5-$10 a day can drive traction if you're targeting the right audience. And speaking of targeting-this is where paid ads really shine. You can get incredibly specific: demographics, location, job titles, interests, even behaviors like "people who engaged with your Instagram account in the last 30 days." Don't waste your money shouting into the void-focus on putting your message in front of the people who are most likely to care.

And always-*always*-tie your ad to a specific goal. Are you trying to grow your email list? Promote a new service? Drive traffic to a webinar registration? Make sure every ad has a clear, actionable next step. If you're just boosting to "get more eyeballs," you'll spend money without seeing real returns.

Want to level up your results even more? Pair your ads with an email campaign or follow-up funnel. For example, run an ad that promotes a free downloadable resource, then follow up with a welcome sequence that nurtures the lead and introduces them to your offer. That's how you turn a click into a conversion-and a conversion into a customer.

And don't forget about retargeting. Most people don't take action the first time they see your brand. Retargeting lets you circle back to people who visited your site, watched your video, or engaged with your content but didn't follow through. It's like giving them a friendly nudge and saying, "Hey, still interested?" And more often than not, they are.

The golden rule? Treat paid social as an amplifier, not a substitute for good content. If your messaging, branding, and targeting aren't on point, no ad spend in the world will save it. But if you've done the foundational work-established your why, nailed your audience, crafted content that resonates-ads can help you scale that impact in a smart, sustainable way.

So when should you pay to play? When you've got something worth saying, something worth promoting, and a plan to back it up. Then? Turn up the volume.

Crisis Management: When Social Gets Weird

It happens. Someone posts a negative comment. A typo goes live. A post misses the mark. Don't panic-*respond*.

Own your mistakes. If you messed up, say so. A simple, "You're right, we missed the mark on this one. We appreciate the feedback and are making changes," goes a long way. No PR spin. No lawyer-approved fluff. Just honest, human accountability.

Transparency builds trust. You don't have to explain every detail, but letting your audience see that you're listening and adjusting shows maturity and integrity. It also demonstrates that your brand is made up of real people-people who care, who learn, and who are willing to do better.

Sometimes the weirdness doesn't come from you-it comes at you. Negative comments, passive-aggressive digs, spammy replies, or full-on trolling. Not every message deserves your energy, but some do require a response.

Here's a good rule of thumb:

- If it's a legitimate complaint, respond publicly and solve the issue privately.
- If it's a misunderstanding, clarify with kindness.
- If it's someone looking for a fight, don't give them one.
- If it's spam or offensive nonsense-delete, block, move on.

It helps to have a simple internal policy or checklist in place for your team: what to respond to, what to escalate, and what to ignore. That way, in the heat of the moment, you're not scrambling-you're steady.

And if something really blows up? Don't go silent. Going dark when the heat's on feels like hiding. Instead, acknowledge what happened, share what you're doing to fix it, and keep communicating. Most people don't expect perfection. But they do expect professionalism. And those who stick the landing after a stumble often come out stronger than before.

In fact, a well-handled crisis can actually *build* loyalty. Why? Because people relate to brands that are real. Owning a mistake makes you human. Fixing it makes you credible.

So yes, social can get weird. But weird doesn't have to be bad. With empathy, humility, and a solid response game, even the worst day on the internet can become a chance to reinforce your values-and earn long-term trust.

Staying Human in a World of Algorithms

The algorithm changes. Platforms evolve. Trends come and go. But one thing always works: being human.

People crave connection. They follow people and brands who make them feel something. So whether you're telling stories, sharing lessons, celebrating wins, or admitting missteps-keep it real.

Authenticity beats perfection every time. And in a world of polished highlight reels, being real is your biggest superpower. In the ever-shifting landscape of the internet, where algorithms dictate visibility, social media platforms rise and fall, and trends emerge and vanish with dizzying speed, a fundamental human desire remains constant: the yearning for authentic connection. Our very nature compels us to seek out relationships and communities that resonate with our emotions, offering feelings of inspiration, understanding, joy, and belonging. In this dynamic digital world, the act of sharing – whether it's personal narratives, helpful advice, positive updates, or even acknowledging our vulnerabilities – hinges on the crucial element of genuine expression. While the online sphere often presents an illusion of flawless perfection, it is authenticity that truly cuts through the noise. Sincerity fosters trust, creating a foundation for lasting engagement and loyalty. By embracing honesty and revealing our true selves, we distinguish ourselves from the homogenous online crowd and cultivate a meaningful following. Ultimately, in an environment saturated with artificiality and carefully curated personas, the power of being real serves as a unique and invaluable advantage, enabling us to forge deeper, more meaningful connections.

Chapter 8

Content Galore

Content isn't just king-it's the entire royal court. It's the words you say, the images you share, the videos you post, and the story you tell every time someone interacts with your brand online. Without content, your website is a skeleton. Your social media, silent. Your emails, empty. Content is what gives everything else substance-and more importantly, *soul*.

In this chapter, we'll unpack how to create, organize, repurpose, and distribute content that not only sounds good but actually works. Because content isn't just about expression-it's about *conversion*.

What Makes Content Work?

Let's start by getting one thing straight: good content isn't just a pretty quote card with a trendy font or a blog post stuffed with keywords and vague advice. That kind of fluff might look nice in your feed, but it doesn't move the needle. Good content has a job-and it knows exactly what that job is.

At its core, content should *do* something. It should educate, inspire, entertain, convert, or connect. Ideally, it does more than one of those things at the same time. A great piece of content might teach your audience something new, make them smile, and subtly nudge them toward clicking that "Book Now" button-all in one go. But at the very least, it should have *purpose*.

When you're creating content, think like a builder. What's the function of this piece? Are you trying to simplify a concept your audience struggles with? Build trust by telling a story? Show off your expertise? Spark a conversation? Drive people to your site? Every piece of content should have a role in your overall ecosystem-and if it doesn't, it probably doesn't need to exist.

Because here's the truth: your audience can smell filler. They know when a post was created just to check a box. You know the type-those vague inspirational quotes that sound like they were generated by a robot doing yoga.

The generic "Happy Friday!" posts with no real thought behind them. These don't build trust. They don't build community. And they definitely don't build conversions.

What they do build is scroll fatigue.

But when your content is intentional-when it's crafted with a goal, a message, and a clear point of view-it stands out. It becomes magnetic. It makes people pause, read, click, think, share, save, or respond. That's when you know you're onto something.

So before you hit publish on anything, ask yourself:
 What is this piece of content *for*?
 Who is it *for*?
 What do I want them to *do* or *feel* after seeing it?

If you can't answer those questions, it's time to go back to the drawing board. Because in today's crowded digital space, clarity and purpose aren't just nice to have-they're the difference between content that gets ignored and content that *actually works*.

Know Your Pillars

Creating content gets easier when you're not reinventing the wheel every time you sit down to post. Let's face it-staring at a blinking cursor with zero direction is the fastest way to fall into a scroll hole instead of actually creating something. That's where content pillars come in to save your sanity.

Think of content pillars as your brand's signature talking points. They're the 3 to 5 themes or categories that you circle back to consistently. These are the topics your audience comes to *expect* from you-and the ones that align most naturally with your expertise, your values, and the things your business actually *offers*. They're not random-they're repeatable, relevant, and rooted in what you want to be known for.

Let's say you're a personal trainer. Your pillars might be:

- **Nutrition** – Recipes, grocery tips, food myths busted.
- **Motivation** – Pep talks, transformation stories, mental health and mindset.

- **Workout Tips** – How-to videos, form corrections, fitness routines.
- **Client Wins** – Before-and-afters, testimonials, day-in-the-life with clients.

Everything you post fits under one of those umbrellas. Not only does this give your audience a sense of consistency, but it also makes your life easier. You're not starting from scratch-you're just plugging into one of your pillars and building from there.

Or maybe you're running a SaaS company. Your pillars might look like:

- **Customer Education** – Tutorials, FAQs, troubleshooting guides.
- **Industry News** – Thought leadership, trends, commentary on what's happening in your space.
- **Product Updates** – New features, improvements, user hacks.
- **Team Culture** – Behind the scenes, employee spotlights, company values in action.

See how different those are from the trainer's pillars? And yet the logic is the same: pick a few key areas that feel authentic and useful to both you and your audience, and lean into them.

Your content pillars become your creative framework. Planning your calendar becomes more like filling in blanks than pulling ideas out of thin air. Want to post three times this week? Easy-one motivational quote under your mindset pillar, one helpful tip from your education pillar, and one behind-the-scenes story that connects to your culture or mission. Done.

Plus, having defined pillars helps keep your messaging on brand. If a topic doesn't fit any of your pillars, it's probably not something you need to post about. It's a filter that helps you stay focused, stay relevant, and stay consistent.

So take a little time to define your 3 to 5 core content pillars. Write them down. Keep them where you can see them when you're brainstorming or creating. You'll be amazed how much easier content creation becomes when you're not reinventing the message every single time-you're just rolling it forward with purpose and personality.

Types of Content That Drive Results

Let's break down the major players in your content playbook:

Blogs: Your Long-Form MVP for SEO and Authority

Blogs are the OGs of content marketing-and they're not going anywhere. Why? Because Google *loves* them, and so do people who want a little more substance than what they can get from a tweet or reel. Blogs are where you can unpack an idea, answer common questions, or go deep on topics that matter to your audience.

Want to boost your search rankings? Create blogs built around relevant keywords. Want to be seen as an expert? Share your insights in lists or bullets, how-tos, or opinion pieces. Just remember: people skim. Use subheadings, bullet points, short paragraphs, and bolded takeaways. The goal is to make it as easy as possible for your audience to get the info they need without getting bored.

Videos: Your High-Energy Crowd-Pleaser

If content formats had a popularity contest, video would win prom king and queen. Short-form, long-form, vertical, square, live-it's all working right now. Video puts a face and voice to your brand, and nothing builds trust faster than seeing a real human on camera.

Use video for quick tips, product demos, how-to tutorials, customer success stories, or behind-the-scenes footage. Instagram Reels, TikToks, YouTube Shorts-they all offer huge organic reach when done right. Don't worry about fancy gear. Your phone + natural light + a little energy is all you need to start.

Podcasts: For Deep Connection and Thought Leadership

Podcasting isn't just for true crime fanatics or Silicon Valley startups. It's a phenomenal format for long-form storytelling, interviews, and casual-but-valuable-conversations. It allows you to go deeper with your audience, share insights in a more personal way, and build authority over time.

The best part? People can listen while driving, walking, cooking-basically anywhere. You become part of their routine, and that breeds trust. If you're not ready to launch your own, start by guesting on others. It's a great gateway into the medium.

Emails: The Unsung Hero of Your Content Arsenal

Don't underestimate the inbox. Email may not be flashy, but it's where conversions often happen. This is your chance to speak directly to someone who already raised their hand to hear more from you. No algorithm standing in the way.

Use email to nurture relationships, provide exclusive value, share updates, or make personal offers. Whether you're sending weekly tips, monthly newsletters, or a sales sequence, treat your list like VIPs-not just leads. Pro tip: your subject line matters more than your first sentence. If it doesn't get opened, the rest doesn't matter.

Social Posts: The Bread and Butter of Daily Content

Social is where you stay top of mind. It's where people interact with your brand casually, quickly, and often. And because of that, it's also where your content needs to be your most engaging and bite-sized.

You've got options: carousels for storytelling or education, reels and TikToks for reach, static posts and memes for relatability, and stories for real-time connection. Vary the format, but keep the voice consistent. And remember: not everything has to sell. Sometimes you're just showing up to be part of the conversation.

Webinars & Workshops: For Education and Lead Gen.

If you're looking to establish expertise, grow your list, or prep an audience for a launch-this is your move. Webinars and live workshops let you deliver tons of value up front while warming up your audience for a next step, whether it's a course, service, or deeper engagement.

They also create urgency and exclusivity: "Join us live on Wednesday" has way more pull than "Check out this post sometime." You can later repurpose recordings into clips, blog recaps, or gated content to stretch their shelf life.

Infographics & Guides: Visuals That Simplify and Share

Sometimes words alone won't cut it. When you need to explain a process, visualize data, or just give people an at-a-glance resource-infographics and guides shine. They're snackable, saveable, and highly shareable, which makes them great for reach and re-use.

A well-designed infographic can take a blog's worth of insight and make it accessible in 30 seconds. Bonus: they also make for great downloadable lead magnets or pins on visual platforms like Pinterest.

Choose formats that fit your strengths, then adapt based on platform and audience behavior.

Content That Matches the Buyer Journey

Let's retire the old-school funnel once and for all. Buyers don't move in a straight line from awareness to consideration to decision. Not anymore. These days, the journey looks more like a flywheel-or better yet, a tornado of tabs, bookmarks, DMs, and "let me circle back on this."

They bounce between your Instagram post and a Google search. They skim a blog, then vanish for a week. They see a testimonial, then binge your YouTube videos at 11pm. It's not linear-it's layered. And that means your content strategy needs to support that.

Welcome to the **Content Pillar Loop**-a modern, always-on approach to digital content that meets people wherever they are in the moment. It's not about dragging buyers through a funnel. It's about showing up with the right kind of content at the right time, consistently, across the right channels.

Let's break down the five core pillars of this circular journey:

Trust: The Foundation of Every Click

Trust is earned before anything else. If your audience doesn't believe you're credible, nothing else matters. And trust isn't built through flashy sales pages-it's built through consistency, transparency, and social proof.

Trust-building content includes:

- Reviews! If your business relies on business listings for your prospective buyers and clients to reach you, you need to be getting as many good reviews as possible, on any platform you can.
- Testimonials with real faces and outcomes
- Case studies that show the journey, not just the results
- Founder stories and behind-the-scenes posts
- Third-party validation (awards, certifications, press)

Trust isn't a one-and-done box to check-it's a layer that needs to exist across every touchpoint. People need to feel like they know you *before* they buy from you.

Education: Because Smart Buyers Are Confident Buyers

People don't want to be sold-they want to feel smart about their decision. When your content teaches, simplifies, or demystifies, it creates confidence. Confidence closes deals.

Education content includes:

- Blog posts that answer real questions (not just SEO bait)
- Short-form video tutorials and explainers
- Webinars, guides, and comparison breakdowns
- FAQ pages that are actually helpful, not just legalese

Educated buyers don't ghost-they convert. Especially when they feel like you've already helped them before they've paid you a dime.

Proof: Show, Don't Just Tell

As mentioned in the first section, we live in a review-obsessed world (catching a trend?). From dinner spots to software tools, people want proof that your thing works *before* they give it a shot. That means showing results, outcomes, and real-world success stories.

Proof content includes:

- Before-and-after stories (visuals help!)
- Screenshots of results, stats, or metrics
- User-generated content (especially if it feels organic)
- Case studies with a narrative arc-problem, process, payoff

People don't trust brands-they trust *other people*. So let your community speak for you.

Clarity: Make the Next Step Obvious

Confused people don't buy. They bounce. Your offer might be amazing, but if it's buried under jargon, unclear pricing, or six different CTAs, you're losing the sale. Clear content is kind (easy to read) content.

Clarity content includes:

- Simple landing pages with one job to do
- Clear pricing breakdowns with context
- Visual process overviews (how it works, step-by-step)
- Straightforward CTAs that guide people, not guilt them

Remember: you're not writing to impress-you're writing to *guide*. The fewer question marks your buyer has in their head, the closer they are to clicking "Let's go."

Connection: Make Them Feel Seen

This is the soul of your content strategy-the stuff that makes people feel like you "get" them. When buyers feel emotionally aligned with your brand, they're not just buying a product. They're buying into an experience, a perspective, or a movement.

Connection content includes:

- Relatable social posts ("You too?!" moments)
- Brand values, origin stories, culture content
- Opinionated takes on your industry or niche
- Behind-the-scenes slices of real people doing real work

People want to do business with brands that feel human. So talk like one. Show up. Share your quirks. Be real.

This Isn't a Sequence-It's a System

Here's the shift: your audience doesn't move from trust to education to clarity in order. They jump between them based on mood, timing, or even what shows up in their feed that day. That's why this is a **loop,** not a ladder. And your content has to live in all five of these zones-all the time.

Your job isn't to push people down a funnel. It's to build a system that makes them feel seen, supported, and confident-*wherever* they are in their journey.

The beauty of this model? It works across platforms, across industries, and across buyer types. Whether someone's brand new or just needs that last nudge, you've got content in place that serves them.

So ditch the funnel. Build the flywheel. And let your content work like a magnet, not a megaphone.

The Content Calendar: Your Sanity Saver

Flying by the seat of your content pants? Constantly posting last-minute? Staring at a canvas like it's a blank interrogation room? Yeah... it's time to stop the chaos. You don't need to be a Type A calendar wizard to get organized-you just need a system that makes content *less* stressful and *more* strategic.

That's where a content calendar comes in. Think of it as your brand's editorial GPS. It keeps you consistent, intentional, and way less likely to forget that you were supposed to post about that big promo… yesterday.

A content calendar helps you:

- **Stay consistent.** This is the name of the game. Consistency builds trust, familiarity, and that wonderful "I keep seeing you everywhere" effect. A calendar keeps your brand voice from ghosting.
- **Plan around launches or promos.** Got a course opening soon? New product drop? Speaking at a conference? Don't wing it. A calendar lets you reverse engineer your content so you're building momentum instead of scrambling for hype last-minute.
- **Maintain variety.** Without a plan, you'll fall into content ruts. Same style. Same message. Same format. With a calendar, you can zoom out and

see the mix: Are you educating enough? Engaging? Showing proof? Selling?

- **Avoid last-minute stress.** Ever tried writing a witty caption while hangry on a Tuesday night? Yeah. Not fun. Planning ahead means you're creating from strategy–not panic.

Your Calendar Doesn't Need to Be Fancy

You don't need an expensive platform to get started. Tools like **Trello**, **Notion**, **Airtable**, or even a good ol' **Google Sheet** can do the job just fine. What matters is what goes *into* it.

At a minimum, track the following:

- **Post date:** When it's going live.
- **Platform:** Where it's going (Instagram? LinkedIn? Email?).
- **Format:** What type of content it is (Reel, carousel, blog post, short video, email, etc.).
- **Topic:** What's it about? What pillar does it support? (Remember your Education, Trust, Proof, etc.)

- **Goal:** Why are you posting this? Engagement? Clicks? Traffic? Lead gen? Pick one and build around it.

Once you've got those fields mapped out, you're not guessing anymore. You're executing with purpose.

Batch Like a Boss

Want to really save time (and your sanity)? Batch your content creation. This means blocking time to work on one type of task across multiple posts, rather than jumping between formats and platforms like a caffeinated squirrel.

Here's how it can look:

- **Monday:** Outline blog posts or email newsletters.
- **Tuesday:** Film short-form videos or record podcast clips.
- **Wednesday:** Design visuals or reels.
- **Thursday:** Schedule everything and polish captions.

- **Friday:** Sip coffee and feel smug knowing you're weeks ahead.

Batching keeps you in flow. You're not constantly task-switching, which kills productivity. Instead, you're getting into a groove and knocking out a week (or even a month!) of content without burning out.

And hey-if a brilliant idea strikes in real time, great! Post it. Spontaneity still has a place. But the goal of your calendar is to give you structure, so you don't *need* inspiration to stay visible.

Repurpose Like a Pro

You don't need to create fresh content for every channel. Repurpose what you already have.

Turn a blog post into:

- A Twitter thread
- An Instagram carousel
- A YouTube script
- A lead magnet checklist

- A podcast talking point

One strong piece of content can generate five or more spinoffs. Think less about creation, more about transformation.

Tone and Consistency

Your brand's voice should shine through every piece of content. Whether you're writing a blog or captioning a TikTok, it should *sound* like you.

- Keep your tone aligned with your brand traits (e.g., cheeky, thoughtful, bold)
- Use language your audience actually uses
- Avoid whiplash-don't sound corporate in one post and unhinged in the next (unless that *is* your thing)

Consistency builds trust. People start to expect a certain rhythm, voice, and style-and that's a good thing.

The Storytelling Framework

Great content tells a story. Your audience isn't scrolling social media or reading your blog for a lecture. They're looking for connection, meaning, value-or at the very least, something that doesn't bore them to tears. That's why great content, no matter how short, *tells a story*.

You don't need to be Hemingway. You just need to follow a simple narrative structure that taps into how our brains are wired. Whether it's a five-paragraph blog post or a single LinkedIn update, storytelling grabs attention and drives action way better than a wall of facts or a hard sell ever will.

Here's a framework that works almost every time:

Hook – Grab Their Attention (Fast)

We live in the age of goldfish-level attention spans. If your first sentence doesn't spark curiosity, strike a nerve, or stop the scroll, the rest of your post may as well not exist.

Your hook could be:

- A bold statement: "Marketing without data is just guessing in a suit."
- A juicy question: "What's the one thing most business owners forget on their website?"
- A relatable moment: "Ever hit publish on a post and immediately cringe?"

This is your first impression-don't waste it on filler. Come in hot, then earn the read.

Problem – Make the Reader Feel Seen

Once you've got their attention, you need to prove you *get* them. This is where you hold up a mirror and describe a challenge or frustration your audience is facing. Not in a "look how broken you are" way, but in a "yep, been there too" kind of way.

When you articulate their problem better than they can, they automatically trust that you might have the solution.

Example:

"Most business owners spend hours writing social content, only to hear crickets when they post. It's not because your offer sucks-it's because your content doesn't make people care yet."

Now they're nodding. Now they're listening.

Solution – Offer Your Take, Tip, or Method

This is where you swoop in with your value. It could be a mindset shift, a quick win, or a fresh perspective on a common problem. You're not solving world peace-you're just showing them the next step forward.

The trick? Be generous, not vague. Give them something real.

Example:
"Instead of listing your services, tell a short story. Start with a problem your client had, then show how your process helped them. People don't buy features-they buy outcomes."

You're positioning yourself as helpful, not pushy. That's magnetic.

Result – Paint the After-Picture

Want people to take action? Show them what life looks like *after* your tip or insight is applied. This is where you add a little transformation magic. Make them feel the benefit.

Example:
"When you shift your content from 'here's what I offer' to 'here's how it helps,' engagement goes up–and so do conversions. Because now your audience sees themselves in your story."

It's not just about explaining what to do. It's about showing what's possible when they do it.

CTA – Tell Them What to Do Next

If you don't give people a next step, they'll do nothing. Not because they didn't like your post-but because you didn't tell them what to do with it.

Your call-to-action doesn't need to be pushy-it just needs to exist. Think of it as closing the loop.

It could be:

- "Try this on your next post and tag me if it works."
- "Want the full checklist? DM me 'content' and I'll send it over."
- "Save this so you don't forget it next time you're stuck."

It can be soft. It can be bold. But it has to *be there*.

Engagement Is Content Too

Here's something most brands miss: the content doesn't stop when you hit "post." In fact, some of the most powerful moments happen *after* the post goes live.

Comments, replies, DMs-this is where your brand personality really shows up. And if you treat those moments like an afterthought, you're missing major opportunities to connect.

Think about it: your response to a comment can often get more visibility than the original post, especially on platforms like LinkedIn and Instagram where engagement boosts reach. A clever comeback, a heartfelt reply, even a simple "thank you!" can spark a ripple effect.

So here's the rule: **don't ghost your audience.**

- **Reply like a human.** No canned responses. No robotic "Thanks for your message." Talk like you would in real life. Be conversational. Be curious. Be kind.
- **Ask questions back.** Turn one comment into a mini-conversation. Does someone say they love your post? Ask what part stood out. Someone shares a success story? Celebrate it with them.
- **Use emojis, gifs, humor-if it fits your brand sparingly.** These little touches go a long way in

showing you're not just a faceless account. But please... Please do not go overboard where it looks like your cat walked on your device with the emoji keyboard open. One or two go a long way.

DMs matter too. That's often where the real stuff happens-questions, leads, feedback, partnerships. Treat that inbox like the VIP room of your brand. Prompt, thoughtful replies build relationships that last.

The best part? This kind of micro-engagement is *sticky*. It builds community. It makes people feel seen. And it creates that "I love this brand and the people behind it" energy that no ad campaign can buy.

So yes, your next viral moment might not be a slick reel or a perfectly worded blog-it might just be a funny reply to someone's comment.

Don't just *post* content. *Be* the content. Every interaction is a chance to reinforce who you are and why you're worth sticking with.

Content and Community

Content should spark conversation-not just broadcast. People want to be part of something, not just watch from the sidelines. That's why your content shouldn't just broadcast-it should *invite*. Spark a conversation, get people clicking, reacting, responding, and-ideally-*participating*.

The best content isn't always the flashiest-it's the most interactive. It makes your audience feel like they're in the room with you, not just watching through a window. That's where the magic happens.

Here are a few ways to make your content feel more like a hangout and less like a monologue:

- **Polls**: Easy, quick, and addictive. Whether it's "Which logo concept do you like best?" or "Tacos or burritos?" polls make people pause-and participate. Bonus: it gives you insights you can actually use.
- **AMA (Ask Me Anything) Sessions**: Open the floor. Whether it's in Stories, a livestream, or a post, give

your audience a chance to pick your brain. This builds authority *and* approachability.

- **Challenges**: Invite your community to take action with you. A 5-day tip challenge. A user-generated content prompt. A "post your workspace" callout. People love to join movements-give them a low-friction way in.

- **Contests**: Giveaways still work-but only if they're relevant and valuable to *your* audience. Ask for a comment, a share, a story reply. Keep the rules simple, the reward worthwhile, and the tone on-brand.

- **Live Q&As**: Hop on Instagram, Facebook, or YouTube Live and answer questions in real time. Even a 10-minute live session builds intimacy. Pro tip: prep a few questions in advance so you're not staring at the screen waiting for someone to type.

Why does all this matter? Because interactive content shifts the power dynamic. You're not just talking *at* people-you're co-creating with them. It's a dialogue. And that's what builds community, trust, and serious brand loyalty.

The more your audience feels like they're part of the process-not just the target of it-the more they'll root for you, share your stuff, and stick around for the long haul.

So go ahead-start the conversation. Let them in. That's where the real engagement lives.

How Much Is Too Much?

There's no universal "right" amount of content, but here's the sweet spot: enough to stay top-of-mind without becoming wallpaper.

Quality > quantity. Five great posts beat 20 forgettable ones. That said, consistency matters more than frequency. Set a sustainable pace and stick with it. Because if you disappear for weeks, don't be surprised if your audience does too.

So what's a good starting point? Here's a sustainable, low-stress rhythm for most brands:

- **Blog:** Aim for 2–4 posts a month. That's enough to build SEO value, showcase authority, and give you solid content to repurpose across social or email.
- **Email:** At least 1–2 newsletters or campaigns per month. This keeps your list warm and gives you a direct line to your audience that's not controlled by algorithms.
- **Social Media:** 3–5 posts per week. Enough to stay in the feed, maintain visibility, and engage regularly-without burning yourself out.

If those numbers feel like a stretch, dial it back to what's manageable-and then commit to it. A consistent drip of solid content is always better than a flood followed by radio silence.

Start small, build habits, and grow from there. You can always increase frequency once you've nailed consistency. Think marathon, not sprint. And remember: your audience doesn't need more content from you. They need content that matters.

Track It or Trash It

Creating content is only half the game. The other half? Figuring out what's actually working. That's where metrics come in-not to stress you out or bury you in spreadsheets, but to help you make smarter decisions about where to focus your time and energy.

Spoiler alert: likes and views are nice, but they're not the whole story. Vanity metrics might give you a quick dopamine hit, but they don't tell you if your content is *doing its job*. To get the full picture, you've got to dig a little deeper.

Here's what to really keep an eye on:

- **Time on Page (for blogs):** Are people sticking around to read your content, or bouncing after the first paragraph? If your average time on a page is 12 seconds, it might be time to punch up that intro or break up that text wall.
- **Open & Click Rates (for emails):** Your email open rate tells you if your subject line did its job. Your click-through rate shows if the content inside was compelling enough to take action. Both are key

signals-and both can be improved with small tweaks over time.

- **Saves & Shares (on social):** A like is a digital nod. A save or share? That's a standing ovation. When someone saves your content, they're saying "this is helpful." When they share it, they're telling others "you need to see this." That's high-value engagement-and a strong signal you're hitting the mark.

- **Signups & Conversions (on landing pages):** If people are clicking but not converting, something's off-maybe it's the offer, maybe it's the copy, maybe it's the user flow. Don't just drive traffic. Pay attention to what happens once they arrive.

Now here's the balance: data should inform your strategy, not boss it around. This isn't about chasing numbers for the sake of numbers. It's about understanding what resonates so you can double down on what works and phase out what doesn't.

Your gut still matters. Creativity still matters. If you feel strongly about trying a bold piece of content-even if the last one didn't perform-do it. But pair that instinct with insight. That's where the real power lives. Call it *data-driven creativity* or *gut-checked strategy*-either way, when you combine analytics with intuition, your content doesn't just look good. It performs.

So check the metrics. Pay attention to the patterns. But never forget: your content is for *people*, not platforms. And the best strategies are always part numbers, part nuance.

Final Thought: Make It Matter

We don't need more content. We need *better* content-content that connects, informs, inspires, or makes us laugh in a way that feels human. So whatever you create-make it real. Make it helpful. Make it worth the scroll.

Because content might be the voice of your brand-but behind every voice is a person. And your job? Make sure that person sounds like someone worth listening to.

Chapter 9

Reputation Management

Your reputation walks into the room before you do-especially online. Before a prospect books a call, follows you, or even skims your about page, they're doing some light digital stalking. A review here. A star rating there. That mildly dramatic Yelp rant from 2017? They saw it-and they're judging.

In the digital age, your reputation isn't just about what people say over brunch. It's what pops up when someone Googles you. It's the collection of reviews, posts, shoutouts, and complaints-fair or not-that form someone's first impression of you. And since most of that happens without your involvement, managing it isn't optional-it's essential.

Trust Starts Before Hello

Let's get one thing straight: people trust people-but online, they trust what they can see. And that usually means reviews, ratings, testimonials, and search results. Before someone even reaches out, they're quietly piecing together your credibility from what's already out there. If your digital footprint shows consistency, professionalism, and a bit of warmth? They're intrigued. They lean in. But if your online presence looks forgotten, fractured, or full of red flags, it can be a dealbreaker.

Think about it-when's the last time you booked a service without reading a review? Or trusted a company with no Google presence? A polished, positive reputation builds trust faster than any flashy ad campaign. It reassures prospects that others have had good experiences, that you show up professionally, and that you're not going to disappear once they hit "buy."

More than that, a solid reputation boosts your credibility with search engines. It makes you more clickable. It increases conversions. It shortens the sales cycle. Bottom line: trust is the currency of the internet-and your reputation is your biggest asset.

Here's the wild part-your reputation lives in more places than you think. It's not just your website or your Google

Business listing. It's Yelp. It's LinkedIn comments. It's that three-sentence review someone left on Facebook in 2021. It's Twitter threads, Reddit rants, blog post shoutouts, and yes, even Glassdoor if you have a team.

So, do yourself a favor. Open an incognito window. Google your name. Google your brand. See what pops up-and not just on the first page. Click around. This audit isn't to panic you-it's to help you *own the narrative.*

It's Not Just What They Say-It's What You Say Back

Reviews aren't just little report cards-they're ongoing conversations. And how you respond matters just as much as what's being said about you. When someone leaves a glowing review, don't settle for a simple "Thanks!" Go a little deeper. Call out something specific they mentioned-maybe it was the fast delivery, the friendly staff, or how your product solved a real problem for them. Let your tone reflect your brand's personality. Be warm. Be witty. Be you.

Your responses are part of your reputation. People reading your reviews aren't just scanning for stars-they're watching how you interact. A thoughtful, genuine reply can elevate even a five-star review and leave an even stronger impression.

Now, let's talk about the one-star moments. Yes, they sting. But they're not the end of the world. The key? Don't get defensive. Don't try to prove your point in a paragraph. Don't let your ego drive your keyboard. Take a moment. Then respond calmly, acknowledging their frustration without overpromising. A simple "I hear you" goes further than a wall of excuses. Offer to make it right when appropriate-and invite them to continue the conversation offline if possible.

Why? Because the internet loves screenshots. A snarky or combative reply lives forever. And trust me-future customers are watching closely.

Even neutral or slightly confused reviews are an opportunity. Maybe someone didn't quite understand how your service works or left a three-star review with no comment. Still worth a reply. Clarify where needed, show openness, and keep it classy. The way you show up in these moments builds trust not just with the reviewer, but with everyone else silently reading along.

Remember, your review section isn't just feedback-it's content. It's proof. And it's a powerful signal of how you treat your people, especially when things aren't perfect.

Get the Good Word Out (On Purpose)

Let's be honest-happy customers are often silent. Meanwhile, the one person whose latte wasn't hot enough has already posted a 500-word takedown before you've even had a chance to blink. That's why you need a proactive system to encourage your satisfied clients to speak up and share their experience.

Start by timing it right. After a job well done, send a simple, friendly follow-up message asking for a review. Nothing pushy-just a quick "Thanks again for working with us! If you had a good experience, would you mind leaving a quick review? It really helps." And include the direct link to your Google, Yelp, or industry-specific review page. Make it brain-dead easy.

Better yet, build the ask into your thank-you email, post-purchase follow-up, or project completion message. You're already contacting them–it's the perfect moment to gently ask for their feedback while the experience is fresh. And if you've got a good relationship, there's no harm in asking personally. Something like, "Hey, it really helps us out when clients leave a quick note about their experience–would you mind dropping one in when you have a second?"

Keep it simple. Keep it fast. People are more likely to do something when the path of least resistance is right in front of them. And if they forget? No big deal–send one gentle reminder. Often, all it takes is a nudge to move a happy customer from silent fan to vocal supporter.

You can even provide prompts to make it easier: "What did you love most about the experience?" "Was there a specific result you noticed?" "Would you recommend us to others?" This not only makes it easier for your client–it often leads to more detailed, persuasive reviews.

And finally, don't treat reviews as a one-and-done initiative. Make asking for them a consistent part of your workflow. Whether it's after every sale, once a project wraps, or at the end of a successful engagement, asking for feedback should be just as routine as sending an invoice. It's one of the easiest ways to build a reputation that works for you around the clock.

Keep an Eye on the Noise

Managing your reputation isn't a set-it-and-forget-it game-it's an ongoing practice. Think of it as hygiene for your brand's credibility. First, set up Google Alerts for your name and business so you're notified the moment something new is said online. Then go a step further and use tools like Mention, Birdeye, or ReviewTrackers to monitor mentions across platforms, from social media to third-party review sites.

Make it a habit-weekly, biweekly, whatever fits your rhythm-to do a reputation pulse check. What are people saying? Are there new reviews that need replies? Are there questions left unanswered? Treat this like checking your voicemail-it's a basic part of showing up professionally in the digital space.

But don't stop there. Watch your competitors, too. What are their customers praising? Complaining about? Where are they getting featured? Observing your competition can reveal industry gaps, messaging opportunities, and easy wins to differentiate yourself.

Staying informed isn't just about defense-it's about offense. When you know what's being said about you and the landscape around you, you can take smarter, faster, more intentional action. That's not just managing your reputation-that's building it on purpose.

Your Reviews = Free Marketing

Here's the fun part: those glowing reviews? They're gold. Seriously. Don't just let them sit quietly on a third-party site collecting digital dust-put them to work. Think of each great review as a mini billboard that someone else wrote for you, for free.

Add snippets of praise to your website-especially on your homepage, service pages, or near calls-to-action. These bite-sized testimonials reinforce trust right when someone is considering whether to take the next step.

Got a carousel on your homepage? Fill it with kind words. Writing a proposal or pitch deck? Drop in a few client quotes that highlight your strengths.

But don't stop there. Turn these reviews into visuals for your social media-quote graphics, Instagram stories, or testimonial videos if a client's game to be on camera. You can even use audio snippets or screenshots as proof in ads or sales emails. Repurpose glowing feedback into different formats depending on where your audience hangs out.

Have a newsletter? Feature a "client spotlight" section that highlights positive experiences. Or drop a quote of the month at the bottom of your email signature. It's subtle, but it works. Happy words from happy customers never go out of style.

Of course, always keep it classy and real. Don't cherry-pick in a way that feels too polished. Let the language of the review shine through-if someone says you "totally crushed it," use their exact words (as long as it fits your brand). Keep the human tone intact.

Also, be respectful. If a review is particularly personal or detailed, ask for permission before blasting it everywhere. Or anonymize it with a generic job title or initials-just enough to keep it believable and relatable.

The key is this: your reputation isn't just a shield. It's a megaphone. So turn up the volume and let your best advocates help you tell your story. Because people trust people-and nothing sells quite like a happy customer.

Don't Forget Internal Reputation

If you have a team, your internal culture matters too-probably more than you think. Platforms like Glassdoor aren't just used by job seekers anymore. Potential clients, partners, and investors peek at them too. What your current and former employees say about you in those spaces can have a lasting impact-not just on your ability to hire great talent, but on how your brand is perceived externally.

A toxic work culture doesn't stay hidden for long. It leaks-through high turnover, poor morale, and yes, public reviews. And when that toxicity shows up online, it doesn't just hurt your recruitment efforts-it chips away at the trust you're trying to build with customers. No one wants to buy from a brand that treats its people poorly.

So take care of your culture. Be intentional about how your team operates and feels day-to-day. Foster a space where people feel heard, valued, and safe to share real feedback. You don't need to throw pizza parties every Friday, but transparency, support, and basic respect go a long way.

Encourage team members to share their honest experiences-but never pressure them to leave glowing reviews. Authenticity wins. When employees genuinely enjoy where they work, they'll often share that on their own-and that kind of unprompted praise is more powerful than any carefully crafted brand statement.

Because here's the truth: your team is your brand. How they feel, speak, and show up every day is a reflection of your leadership and values. Treat them well, and it becomes part of your reputation-in the best possible way.

When Things Go Sideways

Every brand eventually faces a mess. A negative comment goes viral. Someone misunderstands a post. A past misstep resurfaces at the worst possible time. Whether it's a minor ripple or a full-on wave, one thing's for sure: the worst thing you can do is go silent.

Silence is its own kind of statement-and not a reassuring one. It can look like avoidance, indifference, or even guilt. Instead, take a deep breath. Pause, don't panic. Then step up.

Start by acknowledging the situation. Even if you don't have all the answers yet, let people know you're aware and taking it seriously. That small act of transparency can calm the waters more than you realize. Then, own your part. If there's something you need to apologize for-do it. Clearly, sincerely, without hiding behind corporate speak or vague half-apologies.

Next, explain your plan. What are you doing to make it right? What's being reviewed or changed moving forward? Give people a sense that there's action-not just damage control. This doesn't mean oversharing every internal memo, but being clear and direct goes a long way.

And don't try to outpost the crisis with ten fluffy Instagram Reels or a string of unrelated tweets. One calm, thoughtful, well-pinned response is worth more than 20 panicked posts.

Lastly, remember this: people are surprisingly forgiving when they feel seen and respected. Most don't expect perfection-they expect effort, honesty, and improvement. Handle hard moments with grace and maturity, and you might come out stronger than before. Crisis can be reputation quicksand-or a chance to show the depth of your character. Choose the latter.

Plant Good Seeds Now

Reputation management isn't just about damage control. If you're only thinking about your reputation when something's already gone sideways, you're too late. The real magic happens when you're consistently showing up with authenticity, value, and a little bit of humanity-before anything ever goes wrong.

Think of it like building a bank account of goodwill. Every time you highlight a happy client, every time you respond thoughtfully to a comment, every time you show up with something helpful or kind or honest-you're making a deposit. Over time, that balance adds up. And when something messy does happen (because it will), you've built enough trust capital to weather it with your audience still intact.

So what does building goodwill actually look like?

It means celebrating wins publicly-but in a way that doesn't feel like you're bragging into the void. A case study doesn't have to read like an awards submission. Instead, tell a story. Share how you helped a client go from "overwhelmed" to "on it," or how your product made someone's day easier. Center the outcome, not just your awesomeness.

It means giving your team some shine. Introduce them on social. Show off their personalities, celebrate their milestones, or highlight what they're learning. This not only humanizes your brand-it shows that you care about the people who help make it all happen.

It also means peeling back the curtain. Share behind-the-scenes content, work-in-progress moments, or even the occasional "here's what we got wrong and how we fixed it" post. People love brands that are real, not just polished. Perfection is intimidating. Vulnerability, done well, is magnetic.

And then there's the kindness multiplier: posting the nice stuff others say about you. A sweet DM from a customer? A thoughtful email? A casual compliment in a Zoom call? That's all content-and it builds trust. With permission, share those moments. Not to boast, but to reinforce that other people are getting real value from what you do.

Also, show up for causes and conversations that matter to your brand and your audience. Whether you support a nonprofit, lift up underrepresented voices, or share resources in a time of need, these moments say a lot about who you are. But a quick note-don't do it just for optics. Performative sincerity is easy to spot. Be real. Be consistent. Walk the walk.

All of this builds a brand people root for, not just buy from. It turns you from a service provider into someone they want to champion. And here's the payoff: when the internet throws you a curveball-when the comment section heats up, or a misunderstanding takes off-you've already proven who you are.

The more trust and positivity you build over time, the more resilient your brand becomes when things get tough. Because when people already believe in your character, they're way more likely to give you the benefit of the doubt.

So, don't wait for a storm to start building your umbrella. Create a reputation that protects you before you ever need it-and keeps working for you every day, rain or shine.

Chapter 10

Lead Generation & Nurturing

If your Digital DNA is in good shape-your website looks sharp, your content is compelling, your reputation sparkles-then it's time to flip the switch and put all that effort to work. This is the moment where your brand stops being just something people look at and starts becoming something people actively engage with. Welcome to the world of lead generation and nurturing.

Think of everything you've built-your site, your content, your social presence, your reviews-as the storefront of a really inviting shop. But here's the kicker: if no one's walking through the door, if people are just window-shopping and scrolling past, then all that polish isn't doing what it's supposed to do. That's where this chapter comes in. This is the "open" sign on your virtual front door. This is where curious strangers become warm leads and, ideally, paying and raving customers.

Lead generation is how you attract the right people. Nurturing is how you turn that interest into trust, and eventually, into action. Together, these two things are the engine behind your digital growth. So buckle up-we're going to walk through how to make it hum.

What Is a Lead, Really?

Let's start with the basics. What exactly is a "lead"? It's one of those marketing buzzwords that gets tossed around a lot, but let's strip it down. A lead is anyone-yes, anyone-who has shown even a glimmer of interest in your brand, offer, or expertise. It doesn't mean they're ready to buy today. It doesn't mean they're a sure thing. It just means they've cracked the door open.

This could be someone who downloaded your free guide. Someone who liked a product video on Instagram. Someone who signed up for your newsletter or entered their email for a discount code. Maybe they filled out your contact form, clicked on a Facebook ad, or even just lingered a little too long on a pricing page. The entry point doesn't matter as much as the fact that it exists-they've stepped into your world, and now you have a shot at showing them around.

Here's where people often get it twisted: more leads do not automatically mean more opportunity. If you're just collecting names and emails with zero intention behind them, you're not really building a list-you're just hoarding digital business cards. It's like going to a networking event, grabbing every pamphlet in sight, and walking out without saying hello to a single person. Useless.

The real power in lead generation is in **qualified leads**-the ones who actually need what you offer, who align with your values, and who are actively searching for a solution like yours. These aren't cold, uninterested prospects. These are people who are already partway down the path. Your job? Gently guide them the rest of the way.

It's Not About Quantity-It's About Quality

Let's go deeper into that point: not all leads are equal. Some are cold. Some are warm. Some are red hot and ready to go. But more importantly, some are the right fit-and some simply aren't. And here's the secret most people don't talk about: it's better to have 100 qualified leads than 1,000 random ones.

Why? Because quality leads are people who are not just interested-they're aligned. They're already pre-sold on the kind of outcome you offer. They see the value. They're primed to convert with less resistance and more enthusiasm. These are the folks who don't need to be convinced you're worth it-they just need to feel like now's the right time.

To attract those kinds of leads, you need to start with clarity. That means really knowing who your ideal customer is-not just demographics, but their challenges, goals, preferences, and mindset. Then you tailor your messaging to speak to them directly.

Don't lead with what *you* think is cool about your business. Lead with what *they* care about. Are they trying to streamline their workflow? Save time? Look better online? Make more money? Feel more confident in their decision-making? Whatever that desire is-speak to it.

Messaging is everything. When you write headlines, emails, or ad copy, ask yourself: is this about me or about them? The more your content reflects their thoughts, the more likely they are to lean in. That's how you filter out the noise and pull in the right people.

The Power of a Good Lead Magnet

Now let's talk tactics. One of the most powerful tools in your lead generation toolkit is the **lead magnet**. If you've never used one before, think of it like your digital handshake-your way of saying, "Hi, I can help," in a way that feels immediate and valuable.

A lead magnet is a free resource that solves a real problem, delivers a quick win, or answers a question your ideal customer is already asking. It could be a cheat sheet, a checklist, a template, a short video training, or even a swipe file. The format doesn't matter nearly as much as the function. The goal is to deliver value fast and make them think: "Dang, if this is what they give away for free, their paid stuff must be next-level."

Here's what makes a lead magnet effective:

- It's specific. "Marketing tips" is vague. "10 Email Subject Lines That Boost Open Rates" is better.
- It's targeted. Don't try to please everyone-create something that speaks directly to your niche.
- It's easy to consume. You're not writing a dissertation. You're solving a problem in five minutes or less.
- It leads naturally into what you offer. Your lead magnet should connect to your core service, not sit in a vacuum.

And here's a bonus tip: smaller is often better. You don't need to create a 40-page eBook. In fact, shorter lead magnets convert better because they're easier to use. A one-pager that saves someone an hour is more valuable than a 60-page PDF they'll never finish.

Think about the kind of question you answer all the time. The thing your audience keeps tripping over. Package up that solution in a tight, clear way, and boom-you've got yourself a magnet worth clicking on.

Calls-to-Action That Convert

Once you've crafted a killer lead magnet, your next mission is to get people to actually take the bait. And that's where your Call to Action (CTA) steps into the spotlight. A CTA isn't just a button. It's an invitation. It's a tiny little nudge that can either spark a relationship or fall flat. And when done right, it can be the difference between a curious lurker and a committed lead.

The best CTAs don't just tell someone what to do-they make them want to do it. It's not "Click Here." It's "Get My Free Toolkit." It's not "Submit." It's "Unlock My Step-by-Step Guide." You're giving people a reason. You're offering a reward. You're framing the action as a benefit, not a chore.

CTAs should live everywhere your audience is paying attention. Drop them on your homepage, in the sidebar of your blog posts, at the end of an article, in a pop-up (but for the love of conversions, make it a gentle one), and inside your email footers. Anywhere a user might be thinking, "This is helpful-what's next?" is a perfect CTA moment.

Also, don't be afraid to test different versions. Try A/B testing different phrases, colors, or positions on the page. Even small changes like "Get Started" vs. "Try It Free" can impact performance. Track what gets clicks. Refine what doesn't. This is part art, part science-and the more you experiment, the better you'll get.

One pro tip: your CTA should match the tone and vibe of your brand. If your voice is cheeky and casual, your CTA shouldn't read like a law firm's homepage. If your brand is elegant and high-end, don't go with "GRAB THIS NOW!" in all caps. Match the energy. Keep it on-brand. Make it seamless.

Don't Underestimate the Landing Page

Now, once someone clicks that irresistible CTA, where do they land? Hopefully not on your homepage. Hopefully not on a cluttered, confusing page with a million links and distractions. Hopefully, they land on a dedicated landing page-a single-focus, zero-distraction zone where the only job is to convert.

A landing page is your digital closer. It's the moment when someone is already halfway interested-and now you have to gently seal the deal. To do that, you need to remove every possible obstacle and make the next step feel effortless.

Let's break it down. A strong landing page includes:

- A clear headline that reinforces exactly what they're getting.
- A short subheading or supporting text that adds a little intrigue or urgency.
- A brief chunk of persuasive copy (think benefits over features).
- One beautiful, clean CTA button.
- Maybe a trust element-like a testimonial, client logo, or quick stat.
- And above all else: no menus, no extra links, no distractions.

Think of your landing page as a funnel with no exit ramps. You're not trying to entertain or educate broadly here-you're creating a seamless, focused user journey. They either take the action, or they don't. No rabbit holes.

Also, design matters. Your landing page needs to look good and work fast-especially on mobile. With over half of web traffic coming from phones, your layout needs to be thumb-friendly. Buttons should be big enough to tap. Text should be legible. The whole page should load quickly and look clean on any screen size.

Bonus: you can use tools like Hotjar or Crazy Egg to track how users interact with your landing page. Are they scrolling? Are they clicking? Where are they dropping off? That data helps you refine your page over time.

The goal of a landing page isn't to wow. It's to convert. Keep it simple, keep it focused, and above all-make the value clear.

Nurturing: The Follow-Up That Builds Trust

Okay, let's say someone has officially entered your world. They downloaded your lead magnet. They clicked the CTA. They filled out the form. Amazing! But here's where most brands go off the rails. They either vanish into the digital void, never to be heard from again... or they immediately start hammering the new lead with non-stop sales pitches. Both are mistakes.

The sweet spot? Nurturing. This is the art of continuing the conversation without being clingy. It's the steady drip of value that builds familiarity, trust, and ultimately, confidence in your brand. It's not pushy. It's thoughtful. It's supportive. And when done right, it turns casual subscribers into brand believers.

Nurturing starts with a mindset shift: you're not selling-you're serving. That means showing up consistently, delivering real value, and proving that you understand their needs. Share content that educates, inspires, or solves problems. Remind them that you're here, that you get it, and that when they're ready to move forward, you'll be the obvious choice.

This can happen through a variety of channels-email is still king (we'll get into that next), but don't ignore social touchpoints, retargeting ads, or even good old-fashioned DMs if you've got the right context. The goal is to stay top-of-mind without becoming white noise.

Also, don't treat nurturing like a one-size-fits-all template. The more you can tailor your follow-up based on where someone came from, what they downloaded, or what they engaged with, the more effective your messaging will be. Show them that you're paying attention. That you remember what they asked for. That you care.

Because here's the truth: nurturing is where most sales are made. Not on day one. Not from the first touch. But from the slow, steady rhythm of relationship-building. Play the long game, and your conversion rate will thank you.

Email: Still the Best Tool in the Box

Even in an age of flashy funnels, AI-powered chatbots, and every new social media platform trying to reinvent the wheel, email remains the unsung hero of digital marketing. Why? Because **you own it**. It's direct. It's personal. It's permission-based. And when done well, it builds relationships like nothing else.

Think of email as your brand's cozy living room. It's the space where you invite people in, offer them something warm and valuable, and have a more relaxed, ongoing conversation. It's not about shouting promotions. It's about making someone feel like they're part of something-and that their decision to stay subscribed is a smart one.

Start with a **welcome sequence** that feels human, not robotic. The first email should say thank you and actually deliver the thing you promised (your lead magnet, the free resource, the download, etc.). But don't stop there. Introduce yourself. Share your story. Explain what your brand is all about, what they can expect from future emails, and how often they'll hear from you.

Next comes the value layering. Over the next few days or weeks, offer up content that's helpful, relevant, and timely. Think tips, how-to guides, case studies, customer success stories, quick wins, or thoughtful insights. Each email should answer the unspoken question: *"Why should I keep paying attention to you?"*

And here's the secret sauce-**don't rush the sale**. It's tempting to jump in with a promo or pitch right away, but resist. Build a rapport first. Earn their trust. When the time comes to make an offer, they'll be far more likely to say yes if they already feel a connection.

Also, design your emails with intention. Use clean, mobile-friendly layouts. Include buttons, not just hyperlinks. Make sure your emails look great on phones (where most people read them) and have strong subject lines that invite curiosity instead of clickbait.

Your email list isn't just a bucket of names-it's a relationship-building machine. Treat it like the powerful tool it is.

Segmenting Makes You Smarter

Here's where your nurturing game goes from good to pro level: **segmentation**. It's the art of dividing your email list into smaller, more specific groups so you can talk to people in a way that actually resonates. Because let's be honest-not everyone on your list is in the same place, wants the same thing, or needs the same message.

Imagine this: one person signs up for your "Beginner's Guide to Building a Brand." Another joins from a webinar on advanced marketing automation. Should they both get the same email sequence? Definitely not. That's like sending the same playlist to both a new piano student and a concert pianist.

With segmentation, you can separate leads based on behaviors (what they clicked), interests (what they downloaded), demographics (job title, industry), or even how engaged they are (active vs. silent subscribers). You can then craft messages that speak directly to those groups-more relevance, less noise.

The result? Higher open rates, better click-throughs, and way more engagement. People feel like you "get" them because you actually do. You're showing that you're paying attention and that you care enough to tailor the experience.

The good news is, segmentation doesn't have to be complicated. Most email marketing platforms let you set up segments with just a few clicks. Even basic groupings like "new subscribers," "leads who downloaded X," or "clients" can help you personalize your approach dramatically.

Here's the real kicker: segmented emails generate, on average, **more than 50% higher click rates** than generic blasts. That's not fluff. That's just smart marketing.

If you want to deepen relationships, increase conversions, and cut through the inbox clutter-start segmenting.

Use a CRM to Keep It All Straight

By now, you might be wondering, *"How am I supposed to keep track of all this?"* Enter: the CRM. Short for **Customer Relationship Management**, a CRM system is like your digital Rolodex on steroids. It helps you stay organized, track interactions, and personalize communication at scale without losing your mind.

Think of it as your memory bank. A good CRM keeps tabs on every lead and customer-their contact info, how they found you, what content they've interacted with, whether they've booked a call, made a purchase, or just lurked quietly on your list.

With this level of insight, you're not guessing. You're making informed decisions. You know when to follow up, what to send, and how warm (or cold) the lead might be. That allows you to prioritize your time and messaging in a way that actually moves the needle.

CRMs also help automate things like:

- Welcome emails
- Follow-up sequences
- Lead scoring
- Appointment reminders
- Re-engagement campaigns

And don't worry-you don't need some $10,000 enterprise-level setup to start. Tools like HubSpot, Mailchimp, ConvertKit, or even Airtable offer free or affordable versions perfect for small businesses and solopreneurs. The key is simply to start using something-because spreadsheets and sticky notes won't scale.

Remember, the more you know about your leads, the more relevant you can be. A CRM gives you that visibility. It's like giving your business X-ray vision-and when you can see what's working behind the scenes, you can make way better moves in front of the curtain.

Timing Is Everything

You've probably heard the phrase "right place, right time." In the world of lead nurturing, this couldn't be more accurate-or more essential. Every potential customer is on their own unique timeline. Some folks show up on your site ready to buy today-they've done their research, they know what they want, and they're just looking for a reason to say yes. Others? They're curious but cautious.

They're in research mode, gathering ideas, weighing their options, and simply not ready to commit.

Your job isn't to shove them down the funnel like they're on a conveyor belt-it's to stay present, helpful, and relevant until they decide *they're* ready to move. That's why consistency isn't just a nice-to-have; it's your secret weapon. You don't need to flood their inbox daily or post ten times a day on social media. But you do need to show up regularly with valuable content that builds trust and keeps your brand top of mind.

Think of lead nurturing like building a friendship. You wouldn't call a new friend every day and expect them to hang out, but if you ghost them for three months, that connection fades. Instead, find a communication rhythm that respects your audience's time and attention while keeping your brand in the conversation. Maybe that's a weekly newsletter, a monthly check-in, or a mix of blogs, emails, and socials spread across the calendar.

The key is showing up with value-not just noise-so when the timing is right for *them*, you're already the obvious choice. That's the power of steady presence.

Automate With a Human Touch

Let's be honest: automation is a lifesaver. It allows you to keep in touch with hundreds (or thousands) of leads without burning out or hiring a full-time communication squad. You can schedule emails, segment audiences, track behavior, and even trigger specific follow-ups based on someone's actions. It's efficient, powerful, and totally scalable.

But here's the catch: automation without personality is just digital spam. People don't want to feel like they're talking to a robot. They want to feel seen. That's why every piece of automated content-every email, every welcome series, every check-in-should still feel like it was written by an actual human who genuinely cares.

Start by personalizing the basics: use their name, reference the content or lead magnet they interacted with, and speak to their specific interests or pain points. Then go a step further-inject your voice. If your brand is cheeky, be cheeky. If you're thoughtful and warm, let that shine through. Include short stories, relatable analogies, or even a quick "P.S." that sounds like something you'd actually say in a conversation.

Also, don't rely on automation to do *all* the work. Mix in some manual check-ins, custom replies, or unexpected moments of delight-a handwritten note, a personal video, or a DM that says, "Hey, I saw this and thought of you." That blend of automation and authenticity is what creates real connection at scale.

Bottom line? Automation should amplify your humanity, not replace it. If your leads forget there's a person behind the brand, you've missed the mark. If they feel like you're right there with them, guiding them through the journey? You've nailed it.

It's Not About Selling-It's About Supporting

Let's take a moment to flip the script. Too often, lead nurturing gets tangled up in aggressive sales tactics-countdown timers, pushy language, never-ending discount cycles. But that's not what builds long-term trust. In fact, it can backfire and make people hit unsubscribe faster than you can say "limited time only."

The truth is, nurturing leads isn't about selling hard-it's about showing up to help. When someone opts in to your content, signs up for your list, or downloads a resource, they're not just giving you their email address. They're giving you a tiny bit of trust. They're saying, "I think you might have something that can make my life better." That's a big deal. Your job is to honor that trust-not exploit it.

So instead of blasting them with offers right out of the gate, focus on delivering value. Teach them something. Solve a small problem. Share a helpful story, a useful resource, or an inspiring case study. Anticipate their questions and answer them before they ask. Be generous with your knowledge and sincere in your desire to help. Over time, this builds a relationship that feels less like "marketer and prospect" and more like "guide and traveler."

And here's the magic part: when the moment does come to make the offer-when it's truly the right fit and right time-it won't feel like a pitch. It'll feel like the next natural step in a conversation they already trust. You won't need to push. They'll lean in. Because by then, you haven't just shown them what you sell-you've shown them what you stand for.

Support over pressure. Helpfulness over hype. That's the kind of nurturing that doesn't just convert-it creates lifelong fans.

Chapter 11

Embracing AI

AI isn't stealing your job, but it might steal your audience if you ignore it. The phrase "artificial intelligence" gets tossed around so much these days, it's easy to assume it's either a Silicon Valley buzzword or the beginning of the robot apocalypse. But here's the truth: AI is not just some tech industry toy or futuristic threat. It's a very real, very present tool that's quietly (and sometimes not-so-quietly) reshaping how we connect, create, and communicate in digital spaces.

If you've rolled your eyes at AI or avoided it because it sounds too technical or intimidating, don't worry. You're not alone. But ignoring it now would be like refusing to use Google in the early 2000s because you thought AltaVista was doing just fine (may have just dated myself). In this chapter, we're going to break down how AI fits into your digital persona, why it matters, and most importantly, how to use it in a way that supports your marketing instead of stripping it of all its personality.

Let's be clear about one thing from the jump: AI is a tool. A powerful, scalable, efficient tool. But it's not a magic wand. It won't turn a broken brand into a brilliant one. It won't fix a tone-deaf message. And it certainly won't replace your personality, your perspective, or your presence.

But used the right way, AI can absolutely make your marketing sharper, smarter, and significantly less stressful.

What AI Can (and Can't) Do for You

Before we get into the how, let's zoom out and look at the why. AI is already being used to do things like generate content, recommend products, analyze behavior patterns, predict customer needs, and even suggest the best time to send an email. Sounds futuristic, but it's happening right now, often in tools you're already using without even realizing it.

What AI *can* do exceptionally well is manage complexity. It can sort through mountains of data faster than any human possibly could, identify trends, and help you make smarter decisions about how and when to connect with your audience. It's a backstage crew, not the star of the show. It handles the heavy lifting so you can focus on the parts that require your actual brain.

What AI *can't* do is connect emotionally. It doesn't have empathy. It doesn't understand nuance. It doesn't know your backstory, your values, or your community. It doesn't know that a wink in your copy means sarcasm, or that "just vibing" in a social post is actually a subtle way of saying you're taking a mental health break. Those things are *you*, and they can't be automated.

So while AI can speed things up and even improve certain elements of your strategy, your human-ness still has to lead the charge.

Content Creation: Your New Creative Assistant, Not Your Replacement

Let's start with one of the most obvious use cases. Writing content: blogs, emails, social posts, scripts, ad copy - takes time, energy, and a little bit of magic. But sometimes that magic feels completely out of reach. Enter AI writing tools.

Platforms like ChatGPT, Jasper, Copy.ai, and even the AI writing features built into numerous platforms can help generate ideas, create outlines, rewrite paragraphs, and even mimic a certain tone. If you've ever stared at a blank screen wondering what to write for your next newsletter, AI can step in like the world's fastest brainstorming partner. It won't always nail it on the first try, but it can break the curse of writer's block and give you something to work with.

Here's the catch: it still needs you. AI-generated copy often lacks personality, originality, and sometimes, basic common sense. Think of it like a talented intern. It can crank out a first draft, but it still needs direction, editing, and a few strong notes in the margin.

The smartest use of AI in content creation is to use it for what it's great at: structure, speed, and scale. Let it help you draft content calendars, generate variations of headlines, or repurpose long-form content into shorter, snackable bits. Then you step in and give it the sparkle that only you can add.

Email Marketing: Smarter, Faster, and Less Guesswork

Segmenting lists, crafting subject lines, testing send times, analyzing open rates, it's enough to make anyone hit snooze. Thankfully, AI has entered the chat.

Most modern email platforms now offer AI features that do more than just autofill fields. They can analyze your audience's behavior over time to suggest optimal send times. They can recommend subject lines based on what's worked in the past. They can even auto-generate personalized email content based on user preferences, past clicks, and engagement patterns.

This doesn't mean you should hand over your entire email strategy to the robots. But it does mean you can start relying on data instead of vibes. AI can help eliminate some of the guesswork that causes marketers to overthink every single line of text. It allows you to focus on the message while it handles the math.

Think of AI here as your nerdy best friend who loves spreadsheets and testing things while you handle the brand voice and storytelling.

Chatbots and Customer Service: Be Available Without Burnout

Here's the deal, people expect 24/7 availability now. It's not fair, but it's reality. And unless you have a global support team working in shifts (hi, enterprise brands), you probably can't answer every question, comment, or DM in real time. Enter chatbots.

Smart AI-powered chat tools like Drift, Intercom, and even basic Shopify or WordPress plugins can handle simple customer service tasks like order tracking, FAQs, appointment booking, or content guidance. They can be available all day, every day, without caffeine or PTO.

This isn't about replacing human interaction. It's about filtering and managing the volume so your actual team can focus on the stuff that matters. You don't need to answer "What's your return policy?" ten times a day. Let the bot handle it, and jump in when things get more complex or emotional.

The key to making AI-powered chat work is setting clear expectations. Make sure your bot introduces itself as a bot, has friendly (but not too fake) language, and always offers a way to reach a real person if needed. Used well, AI chat support creates a smoother experience for your audience *and* saves you time and sanity.

Analytics & Personalization: Make Smarter Moves With Less Guessing

Analytics are supposed to help you make better decisions, but let's be honest, they often just make you feel guilty. You log in, see a bunch of graphs and bounce rates, and then quietly close the tab and pretend everything's fine. AI can help change that.

Modern analytics tools now use machine learning to surface actual insights instead of just dumping data in your lap. Platforms like Google Analytics 4, Adobe Experience Platform, and Hotjar's AI features can spot behavior patterns, identify where users are dropping off, and suggest content or navigation improvements based on actual usage not hunches.

Beyond analytics, AI is also powering real-time personalization. That means your website can show different content to different users based on where they came from, what they've clicked on before, or even what time of day it is. Sounds fancy, but recent tools make it surprisingly accessible even for small businesses.

Used well, this kind of intelligence helps you deliver the right message to the right person at the right time, without stalking them or being creepy. It's about being helpful, not invasive. It's about relevance, not gimmicks.

Stay Curious, Not Cynical

Here's the bottom line: AI isn't going anywhere. It's evolving fast, and it's already becoming an essential part of modern marketing. But it's not here to take your job, erase your brand, or strip your messaging of meaning.

If anything, AI gives you the breathing room to *be more human*. It clears your plate of the repetitive, mechanical stuff so you can focus on connection, creativity, and strategy. You don't have to become an AI expert to use it effectively. You just need to be open, willing to experiment, and committed to staying in the driver's seat.

The brands that win in the next five years won't be the ones who automate everything. They'll be the ones who know how to combine the efficiency of machines with the irreplaceable magic of being human.

So go ahead, try a new tool. Automate a thing or two. Test a smarter email sequence. Just remember: your audience isn't looking for a perfect funnel or a hyper-optimized content bot. They're looking for someone who gets them. Make sure that someone is still you.

Chapter 12

Stick to Your Plan

You've put in the work. You've nailed your Digital DNA-built the site, crafted your content, polished your social presence, earned those shiny reviews, and even started seeing leads trickle in. So now what?

Well, now you do something most people forget to do: you stick to the plan.

Sticking to the plan isn't sexy. It's not flashy or trendy. It's not the next big hack or shiny tool. But it *is* the difference between momentum and burnout, consistency and chaos, a brand that thrives and one that fades into the algorithm's void.

This final chapter is all about keeping that digital machine you've built humming along. Because building your Digital DNA isn't a one-and-done project. It's a living, evolving thing. And the secret to making it work for the long haul is this: show up, even when it's not exciting.

Build Rhythms, Not Routines

Let's start with your weekly and monthly rhythm. We're not talking about rigid, minute-by-minute schedules here. We're talking about patterns-simple cycles you can maintain even when life gets messy.

Maybe Mondays are for scheduling your social posts. Wednesdays for writing blog content. Fridays for checking your analytics. Find a groove that works for you and your team (even if your "team" is just you in sweatpants with a to-do list). It doesn't have to be perfect. It just has to be consistent.

The goal here isn't to become a content robot. It's to create sustainable habits that keep your digital presence active without overwhelming your life.

Measure What Matters

Once your systems are humming along, make time to check the dashboard. No, you don't need to obsess over every metric, but you do need to know what's working and what's just noise.

Start by asking yourself: what does success actually look like for you right now? Is it more website traffic? More qualified leads? More email signups? More customer reviews?

Track those things—and only those things—regularly. Set a recurring calendar reminder to review your metrics monthly or quarterly. Use simple tools like Google Analytics, your email platform's dashboard, or even a good ol' spreadsheet. Look for trends. Identify what's working. Ditch what isn't. Rinse and repeat.

Revisit Your Goals Quarterly

Goals are not tattoos. You're allowed to change them.

Every 90 days, take a step back. Look at where you are versus where you want to be. What's changed? What's no longer relevant? What deserves more focus?

Quarterly check-ins keep you honest. They keep your goals fresh. And they remind you that building a digital presence isn't about being busy—it's about being effective.

Create a Content Habit

You've probably heard the phrase "content is king." That's true. But consistency is the kingdom. And most brands fizzle out not because they run out of ideas-but because they run out of steam.

The solution? Make content part of your workflow, not an afterthought.

Try batching. Set aside one day a month to map out your content calendar. Brainstorm blog topics, jot down video ideas, repurpose old material. Get into a rhythm where your content supports your brand goals-without becoming a constant scramble.

You can also create a "content bank"-a stash of evergreen pieces you can pull from when inspiration is low. Think templates, FAQs, testimonials, behind-the-scenes insights, quick tips. Build it now so future you can thank you later.

Stay Flexible (Because Life Happens)

Let's be honest. Sometimes, you'll miss a post. Or a campaign will flop. Or your perfectly planned quarter will get derailed by something unexpected. It happens. Welcome to running a business.

The plan isn't sacred. What matters is the *intention* behind it.

Give yourself grace. Adjust timelines when needed. Pivot when the market demands it. But don't abandon ship just because the waters get a little choppy. Flexibility is a strength, not a failure.

Avoid Burnout by Outsourcing Wisely

You can do a lot, but you can't (and shouldn't) do everything. As your brand grows, one of the smartest things you can do is get help. Outsource the tasks that drain you. Automate the stuff that repeats. Delegate the things that fall outside your zone of genius.

Hire a virtual assistant to help with scheduling. Bring on a freelance copywriter to support blog content. Use tools like Zapier to automate workflows. You're not giving up control, you're giving your energy better direction.

Remember: your time is a non-renewable resource. Spend it on the things only *you* can do.

Protect Your Energy, Not Just Your Calendar

It's easy to fill your schedule with strategy sessions, marketing checklists, and ambitious goals. But if you don't protect your *energy*, none of that matters.

Pay attention to what drains you versus what fuels you. Are you energized after writing content or totally wiped? Do analytics excite you or stress you out? The more you understand your own working rhythm, the easier it is to plan around it.

Take real breaks. Schedule quiet days. Build buffer time between meetings. You're a human, not a machine. And your brand will reflect your energy-for better or worse.

Reconnect with Your "Why"

If you ever find yourself stuck in a rut, go back to the beginning. Revisit your "why."

Why did you start this brand? What did you hope to change, solve, or inspire? Who are you here to serve? Reminding yourself of your mission brings clarity when the path gets blurry.

Write it down. Read it often. Let it guide your decisions. Because your Digital DNA should reflect *who you are*, not just what you do.

Embrace the Evolution

Digital strategy is never done. Your brand will grow. Your audience will shift. New platforms will emerge. Algorithms will change. And that's okay.

The brands that last aren't the ones with the best graphics or the biggest budgets. They're the ones that evolve without losing their essence.

So be open. Stay curious. Try new things. And when something doesn't work, treat it as data, not failure.

Growth is messy. But so is momentum.

Keep Showing Up

At the end of the day, building a strong online presence comes down to showing up. Not just when things are exciting. Not just when the calendar is full or the comments are flying.

But consistently. Intentionally. Honestly.

You don't have to go viral. You don't need 100,000 followers. You just need to be there, week after week, with a message that matters and the commitment to see it through.

Show up for your audience. Show up for your brand. Show up for yourself.

Wrapping It All Up

So here we are. The final chapter. You've built your Digital DNA. You understand your voice, your brand, your ecosystem. You've got tools, systems, strategies, and a whole lot of momentum.

Now your job is simple: stick with it.

Not perfectly. Not without setbacks. Just *persistently*. Because the brands that win aren't always the loudest or the fanciest-they're the ones that kept showing up, refining, and evolving.

You've got this.

Your Digital DNA is alive. Keep it that way.

And remember, this isn't the end. It's just the beginning.

About the Author

Chris has been in the marketing industry for over 20 years with over half of them dedicated to building awesome and clean web experiences and campaigns that are built around solid marketing strategies.

Over 10 years ago Chris started his brainchild of an agency, Curiosity. There was a massive void for agencies that focused on the clients' why and began flushing out a process that is beyond successful over the years. With a passion for experimenting with the "next big thing" he stays focused on making sure that each new marketing campaign is rock solid. Over the years Chris has worked with businesses of all sizes. From individual entrepreneurs and their brands to Large Corporations to include Toyota, Bacardi and many more.

The growing and ever changing internet presents different opportunities and unique solutions for clients of all sizes. Chris has a knack for building the proper Digital DNA based on the needs to help build businesses.